Watchable Birds
of the
GREAT BASIN

David Lukas

Photographs by
Brian Small and Don Baccus

With a Foreword by
Graham Chisholm

Mountain Press Publishing Company
Missoula, Montana
1999

Photographs © 1999 by Brian Small: pages 13 (top, bottom inset), 15 (center) 17 (center, bottom), 19 (bottom), 21 (bottom), 23 (top, bottom full), 25 (center, bottom), 27 (center, bottom), 29 (bottom), 31 (top), 33 (bottom), 35 (top, bottom right), 37 (top right, center full, bottom), 39 (top right, bottom), 41, 43 (bottom), 45 (top inset, center full, center inset), 49, 53 (bottom), 55, 57, 61 (top right inset, bottom), 63, 65, 66 (top left), 69 (top, bottom), 71 (bottom right), 73, 75 (top full, bottom), 77 (top, bottom), 79 (top, bottom), 81 (bottom), 83 (bottom left), 85 (top, bottom), 87 (bottom), 91, 93, 95, 97 (top), 99 bottom), 101, 103 (bottom), 107, 109, 111 (top), 112 (bottom), 115 (inset), 119, 121, 123 (bottom), 125, 127, 129, 131, 133 (top), 135, 137 (top left, top right, bottom right), 139, 141 (top, center), 143, 145, 147, 149 (top), 151, and 153.

Photographs © 1999 by Don Baccus: pages xii, 2, 5, 7, 8, 11, 13 (bottom), 15 (top, bottom), 17 (top, center inset), 19 (top left, top right), 21 (top, center), 23 (center, bottom inset), 25 (top), 27 (top), 29 (top), 31 (center, bottom), 33 (top), 35 (bottom left), 37 (top left, center inset), 39 (top left), 43 (top), 45 (top full, bottom full, bottom inset), 47, 51, 53 (top), 59, 61 (top left, top right full), 66 (top right, bottom), 69 (center full, center inset), 71 (top left, top right, bottom left), 75 (top inset), 77 (bottom inset), 79 (center), 81 (top), 83 (top, bottom right), 85 (center), 87 (top), 89, 97 (bottom), 99 (top), 103 (top), 105, 111 (bottom), 112 (top, center left, center right), 115 (full), 123 (top), 133 (bottom), 137 (bottom left), 141 (bottom), and 149 (center, bottom).

Photograph © 1999 by Arnold Small: page 117.

Front cover photographs: Sage grouse (*Centrocercus urophasianus*); Pueblo Mountains, Oregon © 1999 by Don Baccus

Back cover photograph: Black-necked stilt (*Himantopus mexicanus*) © 1999 by Brian Small

Map © 1999 by Virginia Maynard

Library of Congress Cataloging-in-Publication Data
Lukas, David, 1964–
    Watchable birds of the Great Basin / David Lukas ; photographs by Brian Small and Don Baccus ; with a foreword by Graham Chisholm.
        p.   cm.
    Includes bibliographical references (p.   ).
    ISBN 0-87842-397-4
    1. Birds—Great Basin. 2. Bird watching—Great Basin. I. Title.
QL683.G65L85 1999
598' .07'23479—dc21   99-25750
                                                       CIP

PRINTED IN HONG KONG BY MANTEC PRODUCTION COMPANY

Mountain Press Publishing Company
P.O. Box 2399 • Missoula, Montana 59806
(406) 728-1900

*For the people of the Great Basin,
in whose hands lies the future of
these birds and their habitats*

The Great Basin. Shaded area indicates region covered in this book.

CONTENTS

Birds of Deserts and Open Country 67

Birds of Mountains and Foothills 113

FOREWORD

Many people experience the Great Basin from inside an air-conditioned car traveling along Interstate 80. From this vantage point you see mainly a gray green blur of sagebrush with a mountain range in the far distance. Naturally, there is much more. Any visitor who takes the time to turn off the highway will discover the varied and hauntingly beautiful landscapes that make Nevadans glad to call the Silver State home.

The mountain ranges, secret riparian thickets, playas, lakes, wetlands, and hot and cold springs continue to charm the locals and surprise first-time visitors to the Great Basin. As you might imagine, birding in this landscape is hugely challenging and rewarding.

To me, there is nothing more exciting than hiking out to the edge of a Great Basin playa in late April to scan thousands of shorebirds, including American avocets and black-necked stilts, and searching out the occasional rare shorebird that just might be there. Though snow still covers the surrounding mountains, the valley bottoms echo with the squawks and splashes of migrating and nesting waterbirds.

Although few and far between, these wetlands are amazingly diverse and productive. In spring and fall, more than one million birds congregate in the famed Lahontan Valley wetlands, the Humboldt Sink, and the Ruby Valley. These are world-class numbers.

As summer heats up, the narrow canyons and aspen groves of the mountains provide welcome relief and plenty of great birding. Red-naped sapsuckers, yellow and Wilson's warblers, and numerous songbirds take advantage of the willows, cottonwoods, aspens, and other riparian vegetation to nest.

Huge numbers of waterfowl move through the Great Basin from September through November, a favorite time for many birdwatchers to visit the area. Tens of thousands of eared, western, and Clark's grebes and American white pelicans gather at Pyramid and Walker Lakes as oncoming winter freezes push them south. These Great Basin lakes are terminal freshwater lakes, meaning that the watershed ends, absolutely, with them: and no water escapes the lake except through evaporation. The only other lakes like these are in central Asia. Their uniqueness has created an equally unique fish fauna, such as Pyramid Lake's cui-ui fish.

Winter is quieter but brings northern species, especially raptors. Rough-legged hawks, bald eagles, and short-eared owls congregate here during the winter months. Birders can also see northern shrikes and roving bands of horned larks and robins.

Scientists have a relatively poor understanding of the region's bird life. Scientific expeditions, agency biologists, and occasional birders have collected some information, but we lack a comprehensive account of the Great Basin's birds and their habitats. Toward this goal, the recently formed Great Basin Bird Observatory and its partners launched the Nevada Breeding Bird Atlas, the first attempt to develop a systematic overview of the region's breeding birds. The efforts of more than two hundred volunteers are paying off, as new breeding species are confirmed in the Great Basin and knowledge of the distribution of species and their use of the region's varied habitats increases.

Watchable Birds of the Great Basin is the first general introduction to the region's bird life. David Lukas has created a valuable reference for visitors, beginning birdwatchers, and local people who want to learn more about the birds they see as they go about their daily lives. Even for those who already know the region's birds, this book is worth packing and reviewing as you explore the Great Basin.

I hope too that David's passion excites you, as it has so many others, to take action to conserve the habitats that nourish our region's rich bird life.

GRAHAM CHISHOLM
The Nature Conservancy,
Nevada State Director

ACKNOWLEDGMENTS

I extend my thanks to the many people who have made this book possible. Graham Chisholm has been a great inspiration for his singular contributions to bird study and conservation in Nevada. Larry Neel, Bob Flores, Martin Meyers, Don Baccus, Tavia Cathcart, and many friends from the Oregon Museum of Science and Industry, Audubon Society of Portland, and Malheur Field Station have all made birding in the Great Basin a memorable experience over the years. Graham, Larry, Don, and Tavia, along with Pete Bradley, Carolyn Titus, and Brian Small read early versions of the manuscript and provided invaluable insights. I deeply appreciate Virginia Maynard's time and expertise in producing a Great Basin map. Kathleen Ort has been a wonderful editor, offering generous guidance throughout this entire project. Most of all, I thank Tavia, for she brings joy into my life and loves learning about birds.

Looking towards Pilot Peak at sunrise, Goshute Mountains, Nevada

INTRODUCTION

At the heart of the interior West lies a vast, arid region known as the Great Basin. Here all waters flow inward and none escape to the sea. At its western boundary stretches the Sierra Nevada, and along the east the Rocky Mountains; to the north the boundary crosses southern Idaho along ridges that form the Snake River divide, and to the south an arbitrary line based loosely on vegetation changes separates the Great Basin from the Mojave Desert.

Initially, the Great Basin hardly seems a region for birdwatching. Long hours spent traversing barren wastes on interstate highways reveal few birds. But, as in all desert landscapes, the real action takes place at hidden oases; there, the patient observer discovers an astonishing diversity of birds.

The Great Basin holds pockets of lush wetlands that attract millions of waterfowl and shorebirds. Adjacent tracts of sagebrush are home to inhabitants such as sage grouse, sage thrasher, and sage sparrow. In the surrounding hills, streamside willow thickets resound with the calls of many birds, while high-elevation aspen and conifer forests provide habitat for mountain species. In winter, birds gather in the region's valleys in huge numbers, including migrants from the north and mountain birds trying to avoid the intense cold of Great Basin mountain ranges.

I designed *Watchable Birds of the Great Basin* for those whose curiosity compels them to look closely and to wonder about the many types of birds. This book offers images and descriptions that allow readers to identify the most common and "watchable" species. Accounts of the birds' life histories may answer some of the reader's questions and, I hope, may also spark further inquiry.

Watchable Birds of the Great Basin will appeal to wildlife enthusiasts, birders of all levels, armchair naturalists, families, and tourists, but I also designed it for those who live and work in the Great Basin. The survival of these birds depends on the people who daily care for this vast, enchanting landscape.

The seventy watchable birds in this book range from species that are common and highly visible to those that are unique to the region and are challenging to find. I based this list of species on many years of birding in the region, and fine-tuned it after discussions with other experienced birdwatchers. These watchable birds are a sampling, out of several hundred known species, of what the Great Basin offers. I encourage anyone desiring to learn and see more to refer to the books listed in Suggested Reading (see page 155).

The Great Basin offers some of the most stunning wildlife experiences in the western United States, especially during migration, when a substantial percentage of the birds on the Pacific Flyway cross the region. Malheur National Wildlife Refuge, Lahontan Valley wetlands, Mono Lake, and the Great Salt Lake together attract millions of birds, while dozens of other sites, many barely known, are filled with birds as well. Those who take the time to get to know this region will be richly rewarded.

How to Use This Book

At the heart of this book are seventy species accounts arranged according to the standard taxonomic order of birds and grouped in three habitat categories. While most birds roam widely through a range of habitats, I have attemped to assign each species to a typical habitat to help the reader locate birds in the book.

The Narrows, Oregon

Marshes, Lakes,
and Streamsides

Deserts and
Open Country

Mountains
and Foothills

The three categories of habitats are marshes, lakes, and streamside corridors; deserts and open country; and mountains and foothills. These correspond to wet sites, flat open desert regions, and the peaks and slopes of mountain ranges. Each chapter of this book covers one of these categories, and begins with a short, illustrated description. An icon identifying the habitat appears in the upper left-hand corner of each bird's profile.

Each species account begins with the bird's common and scientific names. Few people pay attention to a bird's scientific name, in part because the language of scientific naming is unfamiliar, but interesting information and history are encoded in these names. To help understand the scientific names, I have broken them into their component parts to show their derivation, in many cases from old Greek and Latin roots. A key at the end of the Introduction explains the abbreviations used in these derivations.

The *Eye-catchers* section suggests some key marks to look for in each species and, where appropriate, marks that distinguish the male, female, and young of the species. These key marks are also evident in the photos that accompany each species account. Whenever possible, try to observe these key marks in the field, for they will help you learn to recognize these birds more quickly.

The *Natural History* section offers a variety of information: descriptions of songs, nesting behavior, foods, or other aspects of a bird's life. Each species is unique in some way, and I have attempted to point out these distinctive traits.

When and Where to See Them describes a pattern of occurrence for each species that includes both habitats and seasons. Birds typically follow a predictable pattern that helps you identify the right habitat to search for a particular species. Knowledge of these patterns is an important part of becoming familiar with a region's bird life.

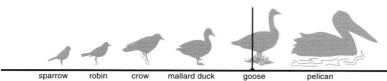

sparrow   robin   crow   mallard duck   goose   pelican

Scale for waterbirds. The vertical bar
indicates a size approximately that of a goose.

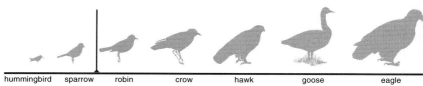

hummingbird   sparrow   robin   crow   hawk   goose   eagle

Scale for land birds. The vertical bar indicates
a size between that of a sparrow and that of a robin.

A graphic scale with a vertical bar indicates the size of each species in relation to silhouettes of familiar birds. Because the shapes and postures of birds vary so much, and affect our perception of size, two different silhouette scales are used: one for land birds and one for waterbirds, that is, birds you will most likely see wading or swimming. These silhouettes are not drawn in accurate proportion to one another, but merely ranked from smallest to largest. These size scales more closely reflect body size and shape than overall length from tip of outstretched bill to end of tail, the usual method of measuring bird size.

How to Watch Birds

Birdwatchers range in intensity from casual observers to passionate "twitchers." Whatever your level of interest, several techniques will further your enjoyment of this activity. Most important, take time to fully observe the bird while it is in view. Nothing detracts more quickly from the enjoyment of your experience than to turn immediately to a field guide, only to have the bird fly away while your attention is distracted.

What do you first notice about the bird? What is its color? Its behavior? Is the bird hunting for food? If so, can you tell what it is capturing? How does it hold itself? Does it stay close to the ground, or sit scanning from a high perch?

After a few minutes, revisit your first impressions of the bird's color. What are the extent and location of prominent colors? Is there a pattern of color on the bird? What color are the wings, belly, and head? Details are crucial to making an identification when you finally turn to a book for help.

The details of a small or distant bird can be difficult to observe, so one of the key tools for birdwatchers is a pair of binoculars. Looking through a pair of binoculars is like falling into a new universe and it takes a little practice to use them properly. High-quality binoculars allow you to observe an amazing level of detail, often to the point of seeing specific feathers.

Learn to scan an area with both the naked eye and with a pair of binoculars; keep your eyes active. Birds may remain inconspicuous until you make an effort to find them. Look for suggestive shapes perched on wires, branches, or atop rocks; watch for unexpected movements; listen for the calls and songs of hidden birds. Over time your senses will become trained and accustomed to this effort.

The best birdwatchers, including experts, take every opportunity to watch birds. There is always something new to witness or learn about birds and their behavior. When you are making your first identifications, extended observations lead to a growing familiarity with new species.

Malheur National Wildlife Refuge, Oregon

Birdwatching Etiquette

Birdwatching is by nature an absorbing activity. In the excitement of the moment, keep several cautions in mind. First, are you disrupting the bird's life by your approach or presence? Second, have you wandered onto private property?

Use your binoculars to maintain a reasonable distance from birds. There is rarely a need to press in closer toward a bird, and you are too close if your presence causes a bird to flush up or to leave a nest. Some species permanently abandon their nests or colonies after being disturbed. Consider what distance is appropriate, maintain a calm, quiet presence, and back off if necessary.

Just as you would respect the home of a bird, respect the rights of private property owners. Owners often grant permission for access to courteous birdwatchers, but do not assume this without asking first. If in doubt, find another site to do your birdwatching.

Abbreviations Used in Species Accounts

E	English
F	French
Gk	Greek
L	Latin
LL	Late Latin
NL	New Latin
OE	Old English
Skt	Sanskrit
Sp	Spanish

Steens Mountain, from Buena Vista overlook,
Malheur National Wildlife Refuge in eastern Oregon

Shorebirds feed at Bear River Migratory Bird Refuge in northern Utah

Marsh habitat at Bear River Migratory Bird Refuge

Malheur National Wildlife Refuge in eastern Oregon

BIRDS OF MARSHES, LAKES, AND STREAMSIDE CORRIDORS

Water in the Great Basin is a precious resource that comes in many forms. Streams flowing out of the mountains are lined with cottonwoods and willows and disappear eventually into desert sands or flow into extensive marshes. Freshwater marshes house a mixture of cattails, bulrushes, and mudflats. Some lakes and marshes are heavily mineralized and support specialized plant and animal communities.

PIED-BILLED GREBE
Podilymbus podiceps

(*Podilymbus,* from *podiceps* [L *podicis,* rump; L *pes,* foot; hence, "rear-footed."] and the old name for loons and grebes, *Columbus* [Gk *kolymbos,* a diving bird])

Eye-catchers: The pied-billed grebe is gray brown, with a short, stout bill, unmarked in winter but with a prominent black ring during the breeding season. Its overall appearance is stouter and shorter-necked than other small grebes. Completely unlike their parents, chicks are vividly striped black and white the full length of their bodies.

Natural History: This solitary and inconspicuous grebe is easily over-looked. When alarmed, it may sink out of sight without a ripple, then resurface and remain motionless with only its head above the water. It controls this ability to sink and resurface like a submarine by compressing feathers against its body. When nesting, it is even more cautious and may not make an appearance if a potential predator is nearby.

Pied-billed grebes vigorously defend their territories by swimming underwater and pecking at the feet of trespassers such as ducks and other grebes. While most grebes are colonial nesters, pied-billed grebes nest in solitary pairs at well-camouflaged sites, often at small isolated ponds. Both members of a pair work on building a nest and raising the young.

Grebes are such highly evolved swimmers that they are essentially helpless on land. For maximum swimming power their legs are situated at the rear of their bodies (hence, *podiceps,* "rear-footed"), but on land they can only lie on their bellies with legs sprawled behind. Unfortunate grebes that mistake wet pavement or ice for a secure pond and settle down will perish, because they depend on water to get airborne. If you watch a grebe take flight (something they rarely do) you will see how they must run across water to pick up enough speed. Although grebes migrate substantial distances, their small wings must make sustained flight a mighty task.

When and Where to See Them: Common but widely dispersed breeder with only one to a few pairs at most sites. Favors well-vegetated and sluggish waters. Small numbers remain through winter so long as waters do not freeze, while migrating individuals leave in September or October and return in March.

Breeding pied-billed grebes lose their black bill ring in winter.

EARED GREBE
Podiceps nigricollis
(L *podicis*, rump; L *pes*, foot; hence, "rear-footed." L *niger*, black; L *collum*, neck)

Eye-catchers: The eared grebe is distinctive in summer plumage, with intense red eyes, jet-black upperparts, and an orange fanlike spray of feathers on the face. Winter plumage is dull—look for red eyes on a gray, scruffy bird.

Natural History: Two major Great Basin lakes—Mono Lake and Great Salt Lake—attract so many eared grebes during fall migration that it is possible to imagine hopping across the lakes on the backs of grebes. The one million grebes stopping at Mono Lake define the term *superabundant*. They can become so fat from feasting on the brine shrimp of Mono Lake that they have to fast before they can fly. After fattening up, grebes continue south to winter in coastal regions and inland waters of the Southwest.

Unlike their large, fish-eating cousins, the western and Clark's grebes, eared grebes relish a diet of aquatic insects. In years when aquatic insect numbers fall, eared grebes may forego nesting at some Great Basin sites, but in good years they nest in dense colonies comprising hundreds of pairs. Nesting seems a haphazard affair: nests are little more than an untidy, flimsy platform of sodden marsh vegetation, which tilts precariously as the bird climbs aboard. At times, the entire colony simply abandons nests, eggs and all, and moves on to another site to rebuild. It is a miracle eggs hatch at all, because they often sit partially submerged in cold water. After the eggs hatch, the parents become protective and frequently hide their chicks within the dense feathers on their backs. When frightened, chicks either rush to their parents and clamber onto their backs, or they dive and swim away with powerful strokes of their abnormally large feet, coming up again under floating plants with only their beak and nostrils showing above the water. As they grow, young chicks from many broods join together in groups of peers. After nesting, most grebes move to lakes with rich food sources to fatten up for the winter.

When and Where to See Them: Found throughout the Great Basin on a variety of waters from April to September. Many stay through winter but the majority head south. Abundant during migration.

Winter eared grebes still show red eyes.

Breeding eared grebe shows orange spray of feathers around face;
after diving (inset), grebes appear bedraggled.

CLARK'S GREBE
Aechmophorus clarkii
(Gk *aichme*, spear; Gk *phoreus*, bearer. Named for William Clark
of the Lewis and Clark expedition)

Eye-catchers: This grebe's long, graceful neck and elegant demeanor
is distinctive, giving it the alternate name swan grebe. Look for the sharp,
contrasting black-and-white pattern along its neck and head, and the
spearlike bill. Once considered the same species as the **western grebe,**
Clark's grebe has a white face and orangish bill, whereas the western grebe
has a dark face and a greenish bill.

Natural History: Large, open bodies of water are the haunts of this
striking grebe and its look-alike relative, the western grebe. Pyramid Lake,
just north of Reno, and Lake Mead, outside Las Vegas, attract large
numbers of both species during migration. The Clark's grebe typically
stays in deeper waters farther from shore.

The millinery and garment trades decimated populations of both these
grebes at the beginning of the twentieth century. President Theodore
Roosevelt stopped this slaughter in 1908 when he established wildlife
refuges at Malheur and Klamath Lakes to protect nesting colonies. Today,
these grebes are once again widespread, and you can hear their loud *kreek*
(Clark's) and *kreek-kreek* (western) calls in many areas. Their nesting
season begins when aquatic vegetation grows high enough to anchor
floating nests, and conspicuous courtship displays ensue. One spectacular display involves a pair swimming side-by-side with choreographed
postures, then springing upright and running across the water together
in a mad, splashing frenzy.

Soon after hatching, young chicks start on a diet of feathers, and
within three days their tiny stomachs are filled with several hundred of
their parents' feathers. This curious diet is common to all grebes, and
adults ingest their own feathers throughout their lives. The feathers may
retard digestion long enough to dissolve sharp fish bones that could
otherwise puncture the grebe's intestines. Fish make up a large portion
of these grebes' diets.

When and Where to See Them: Common breeder on many large
bodies of water, nesting in colonies of tens to hundreds of birds. Resident
from March to October, with some staying through winter, especially in
the southern half of the Great Basin.

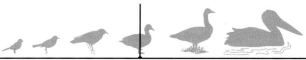

Young western grebes find a safe haven on their parent's back while being fed a small fish.

Greenish bill and more extensive black cap helps distinguish the western grebe.

Clark's grebe

AMERICAN WHITE PELICAN
Pelecanus erythrorhynchos
(Gk *pelekan,* pelican. Gk *erythros,* red; Gk *rhynchos,* beak, bill)

Eye-catchers: A long, large orange bill distinguishes these pelicans from other white waterbirds of the Great Basin. In flight, black wing tips and a 10-foot wingspan are diagnostic.

Natural History: White pelicans are among the most majestic birds of the Great Basin. Solemn, oddly graceful, and awe-inspiring, they capture the viewer's imagination as they circle high in the air in tight, choreographed formations. Sometimes they fly so high that they are only visible when they turn and flash in the sun like white mirrors.

American white pelican populations are particularly vulnerable on their nesting grounds, and there are only about fifteen nesting colonies left in the world. Several of the finest colonies survive in the Great Basin, including those at Pyramid Lake and Great Salt Lake; this makes the region an important refuge for the species. Current threats to colonies include declining lake levels that allow predators access to otherwise isolated nesting islands, and inquisitive humans who scare adult birds away from vulnerable eggs and young.

From their island colonies, parents take turns making feeding runs that may take them over a hundred miles to productive, shallow-water lakes where they can more easily catch fish. It would seem that a 200-mile round trip would be exhausting, but pelicans are master fliers. Their massive wingspans and lightweight bodies, buoyed by an extensive network of air sacs under the skin, allow them to glide effortlessly for hours with scarcely a wing beat.

Unlike their ocean-going cousins, brown pelicans, American white pelicans do not capture fish by diving headfirst into the water. They feed on whatever fish they can catch and get airborne with, using their large throat pouches as dip nets while paddling about on the water's surface. Often a group of pelicans feed cooperatively by lining up to chase fish into shallower water where they are easier to catch.

When and Where to See Them: Arrives back in the Great Basin in early March and stays until October or as late as December. Abundant near nesting colonies, but easily seen throughout the region because of long-distance feeding runs and postbreeding dispersal.

American white pelicans line up to chase fish into shallow water.

Adults in nonbreeding plumage lose the knob on the bill (inset) that breeding pelicans show.

Black wing tips are conspicuous in flight.

WHITE-FACED IBIS
Plegadis chihi
(Gk *plegadis*, a sickle or scythe. *Chihi* may be a South American name for the bird)

Eye-catchers: Once called bronze turkey or black curlew, this ibis appears dark at a distance, but good light reveals its beautiful maroon body with purplish bronze and green wings. A rim of white feathers around the face during the breeding season gives this species its name. The nonbreeding plumage is considerably duller. At all seasons the long, stout, down-curved bill is conspicuous. In flight, the bird's legs stretch back past the tip of the tail.

Natural History: Ancient Egyptians revered the ibis of the Old World as gods, and certainly the white-faced ibis of western North America command attention as well. Their glistening, iridescent feathers are gorgeous in the sunlight, changing hues with each movement. While in flight, white-faced ibis give a curious call, described by some observers as a piglike grunt; this call either adds to or detracts from the bird's mystique, depending on your point of view. With practice, you can recognize ibis at great distances by their unique style of flapping and gliding, and by the way flocks fly in formations that ceaselessly break and shift.

The history of white-faced ibis populations has been more eventful than a carnival ride. Hunting, DDT, and habitat alterations led to declines in these beautiful birds; however, their populations naturally fluctuate widely in response to changing water levels, and they have a strong ability to recover.

White-faced ibis favor tule marshes, where they build nests by bending old stems over to form elevated platforms. Colonies are noisy and active, with ibis constantly arriving and departing for feeding grounds. White-faced ibis commonly frequent flooded agricultural fields, where they feed heavily on invertebrates.

When and Where to See Them: Locally fairly common from April through September; widespread during migration, when they may appear at any moist site. Rarely, may overwinter in the Great Basin. The best places to find this bird are at the great nesting colonies at Malheur National Wildlife Refuge, Lahontan Valley wetlands, and Bear River Migratory Bird Refuge. Also common at Ruby Lake National Wildlife Refuge and at the Franklin Lake Wildlife Management Area immediately to the north.

Ibis use their long bills to probe in the mud for food.

Flooded meadows are a favorite habitat.

The white-faced ibis in winter

CINNAMON TEAL
Anas cyanoptera
(L *anas*, a duck. Gk *kyaneos*, dark blue; Gk *pteron*, wing)

Eye-catchers: The cinnamon red male teal is quite handsome. With practice, you can recognize females and young birds by their slightly oversize bill and by the warm, ruddy tones in their feathers.

Natural History: Few birds on a Great Basin marsh are as beautiful as the male cinnamon teal with his vibrant, deep reddish plumage. In good light, the feathers glow with color and are strikingly offset by bright blue and green patches on the wing (sometimes hidden when bird is at rest, but conspicuous in flight). Glaring red eyes further highlight the male's appearance. These red eyes remain distinctive during late summer, when males temporarily molt into a plain brown, female-like plumage. Females are drab in comparison, but this camouflage helps protect nests and ducklings.

First discovered living at the tip of South America, cinnamon teal were long thought of solely as South American birds. Survey expeditions in the 1850s finally revealed that cinnamon teal also inhabit marshes west of the Rocky Mountains. In fact, they are the most abundant breeding duck in much of the Great Basin, and a large percentage of the North American population spends time here. The closely related blue-winged teal also breeds in the Great Basin.

Cinnamon teal gather in pairs or small groups as they feed on submerged aquatic plants along the margins of shallow bodies of water. More than other species of ducks, cinnamon teal frequent alkaline waters, where they use their long, slightly spatulate bills to strain the mud for insect larvae. Females nest in wet meadows, and groups of ducklings become a common sight by late June.

When and Where to See Them: Common to abundant breeder and migrant in shallow waters throughout the Great Basin. Frequents agricultural drains and alkaline marshes. Rarely winters in the northern part of the region, but a fairly common winter bird in the southern Great Basin.

This stretching cinnamon teal shows the normally hidden wing patch.

Breeding cinnamon teals are one of the marsh's most beautiful birds.

Female cinnamon teal

REDHEAD
Aythya americana
(Gk *aythya*, a waterbird. NL *americana*, of America)

Eye-catchers: Males have a chestnut red head. Smoky gray sides and back distinguish this species from the larger **canvasback,** which also has a chestnut red head but has whitish sides and back. Female redheads are warm brown overall and look like many other female ducks.

Natural History: This tame, easily lured duck has long been a favorite game bird, but habitat loss, hunting, and low reproductive success have led to a precipitous decline in their numbers. Fortunately, several significant breeding areas still persist in the Great Basin, and redheads can be abundant breeders at marshes of the Great Salt Lake, Malheur National Wildlife Refuge, and Lahontan Valley. Many other marshy areas, lakes, and ponds support smaller numbers. Their primary requirement appears to be deeper bodies of water ringed by dense stands of tall, emergent marsh vegetation. Here females build well-hidden baskets of cattails or bulrushes in which to lay their eggs. By human standards, redheads are notoriously poor parents. Females readily abandon their nests, or lay their eggs in "dump nests," unincubated nests where different females leave as many as eighty-seven eggs. When chicks do hatch, the parents make little attempt to protect them and may leave them well before they are able to fly.

Redheads are best known as brood parasites, a bird that lays its eggs in the nests of other birds. While other redheads are a favorite target, redheads also lay eggs in the nests of different species, including coots and bitterns. Perhaps chicks raised by more protective species have a better survival rate than those raised by their redhead parents.

Although redheads dive frequently to feed, they also dabble (tilting forward with their head underwater and rear end in the air) and feed far less on animal food than their diving cousins.

When and Where to See Them: Found in large concentrations outside of the breeding season, often observed resting far from shore on larger bodies of water. Winter freezes send all but a few hardy ones south until March or April, when they return to breed again in the northern Great Basin.

The steepness of the forehead and bill color help distinguish the male redhead from the canvasback.

Male canvasback

Female redheads show the same black-tipped, blue bills as males. Inset: Male redhead in flight

RUDDY DUCK
Oxyura jamaicensis

(Gk *oxys,* sharp; Gk *oura,* tail. NL *jamaicensis,* of Jamaica)

Eye-catchers: The bright blue bill and rich chestnut color of a breeding male create an unforgettable image. Females and birds in nonbreeding plumage are brownish with a variable white cheek patch. The short, thick neck, the broad bill, and the long, cocked tail are distinctive at all times.

Natural History: These small, hardy ducks have so much personality that it is easy to develop a liking for them. They are, in a word, cocky: riding high in the water, bright and alert, their erect tails spread like a fan. Courting males have the curious habit of swallowing air to inflate special throat sacs, then beating their bills against their chests to produce a drumming sound. Often they beat their chests so fervently that they create a frothy bath around themselves. The display ends with a belch as they exhale air. Apparently, it is a hit with the hens because ruddy ducks are very abundant.

Ruddy ducks can become inconspicuous when alarmed. Poorly equipped for flight with only short, stubby wings, they resort to sinking slowly out of sight and swimming underwater away from danger. When forced into flight, they thrash wildly across the water's surface as they struggle to build up enough speed to get airborne.

In the Great Basin, ruddy ducks are common and characteristic birds of deeper permanent waters bordered by tall, emergent vegetation. Here they find a steady supply of aquatic plants and organisms to feed upon, as well as secure, hidden nest sites. In the central and southern parts of the region, where waters remain unfrozen in winter, they are a year-round resident. Outside the breeding season they gather together in compact rafts and seldom associate with other duck species.

Ruddy ducks are one of the few waterfowl species that, like songbirds, alternate between distinct breeding and nonbreeding plumages. Other waterfowl have the same plumage throughout the year (except for a briefly held, late-summer eclipse plumage).

When and Where to See Them: Found on most ponds, sloughs, and lakes at lower elevations throughout the region. Prefers deeper waters, and during the breeding season, sites with tall, emergent vegetation.

*A handsome
suitor*

*Female ruddy
duck in winter*

Male in winter

NORTHERN HARRIER
Circus cyaneus
(Gk *kirkos*, a circle, or a hawk that flies in a circle. Gk *kyaneos*, dark blue)

Eye-catchers: Long, narrow wings, a long tail, and a diagnostic white rump patch identify this bird. It flies low to the ground and holds its wings up in a V. The male is white below and gray above with black wing tips that look like they have been dipped in ink. The female is brown and streaky; the young resemble females but are cinnamon colored on the belly.

Natural History: Northern harriers, once known as marsh hawks, are a characteristic and conspicuous bird of Great Basin marshes. They fly prominently across marshes and fields hunting for small mammals and birds. Although their flight appears deceptively slow and wobbly, they are agile and effective hunters. Northern harriers constantly pull up, readjust, hover, somersault, and dive as they hunt. Like owls, they have a flattened facial disk that funnels sounds to their ears with pinpoint accuracy. A refined sense of hearing is an especially important adaptation for hunting rodents in dense marsh and meadow vegetation.

   More than other birds of prey, northern harriers spend much of their time on the ground, both sleeping and nesting there. Because their nest is so vulnerable to predators, northern harriers take special precautions to hide it in high marsh grasses. In a specialized feeding ceremony designed to keep the nest site secret, the male brings food to the female, who sits quietly on the nest. He drops the food and the female flies up and somersaults to catch it in midair, but then she makes a series of false landings in order to confuse any watchful predator. If disturbed while incubating eggs, northern harriers will abandon their nest.

   In the spring, watch for the male's courtship display of exuberant roller-coaster flights, performed either alone or in the company of his mate.

When and Where to See Them: Common permanent resident across the Great Basin. Numbers decrease at northern locales and increase at western and southern sites in winter, though overall patterns depend on snow depths and temperatures. Most often observed at marshy areas, but also found at agricultural fields, mountain meadows (up to 10,000 feet), and even on sagebrush flats.

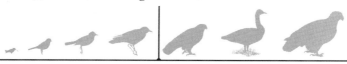

Northern harrier chicks await their next feeding.

Northern harrier female in flight

Northern harrier on low perch in open field

VIRGINIA RAIL
Rallus limicola
(F *rale,* a rail. L *limus,* mud; L *colo,* to inhabit)

Eye-catchers: A secretive, robin-size bird of marshes, often heard but rarely observed, the Virginia rail is recognizable by its gray face, by its long, orange bill, and by the chestnut tones to its body and wings. The **sora,** a close cousin, has a short, thick, straw-colored bill and lacks the chestnut tones of the Virginia rail.

Natural History: Catching a glimpse of this common but furtive species is one of the rewards of birding around the Great Basin. Wet meadows, marshes, and slow-moving streams of any appreciable size are likely to house Virginia rails, but patience is necessary to discover this bird's hidden life. Visit your favorite marsh during the breeding season and you may hear the rail's curious, piglike oinking notes, or loud, clicking *ki-dick* calls. They vocalize often as they go about their activities within thickets of cattails, bulrushes, and tussocky grasses. A fortunate observer will eventually spot a thin, shadowy form slipping through openings as it probes for worms and insects in the soft mud.

Rails are well adapted for marshy habitats, possessing long toes that spread their weight and allow them to walk lightly across floating vegetation without sinking. When pressed, they can also swim and dive, or as a last resort, launch into feeble flight with long legs dangling. Newly hatched chicks leave the nest within hours, already capable of running, swimming, and diving. Within a week these chicks feed self-sufficiently, and their parents soon move elsewhere, leaving the chicks to grow up in and take over the parent's territory. Cold weather eventually pushes rail populations south until the following April. The fact that these feeble flyers migrate is one of the enduring mysteries of the bird world.

The sora is another common but furtive rail of Great Basin marshes. The best way to detect their presence is by their call, a descending whinny. Their life history resembles that of Virginia rails.

When and Where to See Them: Both species are common migrants in April and September, and common summer residents of marshy habitats larger than a few acres. Individual birds may remain through winter, especially in the southern Great Basin.

Virginia rails sometimes leave the security of marsh vegetation to forage.

The sora shows a yellow bill and black mask.

AMERICAN COOT
Fulica americana
(L *fulico*, a coot, related to *fuligo*, soot. NL *americana*, of America)

Eye-catchers: This plump, black marsh bird's contrasting white bill is highly distinctive and visible at a great distance.

Natural History: Coots are an exceedingly common bird of Great Basin marshes and other bodies of water, often present in great numbers. Malheur National Wildlife Refuge hosts up to five hundred thousand during fall migration, and enormous concentrations gather during winter on large reservoirs in southern Nevada.

Besides the *coot-coot-coot* calls that are an ever-present feature of Great Basin marshes, several behaviors make coots memorable. Coots have a comical habit of energetically and incessantly bobbing their heads as they swim. Researchers think this behavior helps them focus on prey items, for coots bob rapidly while hunting for insects and slowly while feeding on plants. Watch for coots splashing wildly with flailing wings and feet while trying to move quickly or take flight.

As soon as ice begins to melt, coots push northward, though their rush to return to old haunts means they sometimes get caught by late freezes and may perish. Pairs mate for life, and both fight fiercely to defend their territory. If weather permits, they remain on this territory year-round. Coots prefer patches of open water surrounded by tall, dense cattails and bulrushes. Within the thick, emergent vegetation, a pair constructs seven to nine floating platforms, one of which they finish and use as a nest. As their eggs hatch over several days, one parent moves the chicks to a separate platform while the other parent continues to incubate at the nest. The reddish orange chicks are extremely capable and readily swim and dive the day they hatch.

Coots feed on many items associated with marsh life. They subsist on aquatic vegetation, but supplement this diet with aquatic insects, snails, tadpoles, and small fish. They even leave the water to graze like tiny feathered cattle on nearby grasses.

When and Where to See Them: Common year-round resident in much of the Great Basin, heading southward in winter only if waters freeze. Fall numbers can be tremendous as young birds join with mature coots on favorable waters.

The coot is a common bird of Great Basin marshes.

Chicks have orange markings.

Adult coot carries a reed back to the nest.

SNOWY PLOVER
Charadrius alexandrinus

(Gk *charadra,* a gully, referring to the nesting site. Specific name honors the city of Alexandria in Egypt, where the first snowy plover was collected)

Eye-catchers: Ghostly pale, this sparrow-size shorebird runs about in a half-crouch, nearly invisible on its alkaline mudflat home. It moves with quick bursts and abrupt stops, and seldom flies.

Natural History: You will scarcely notice this tiny apparition on Great Basin alkaline flats, where its pale feathers blend perfectly with the white alkali crust. The few patches of black about this bird's face, shoulders, and dark legs are hidden from intruders as the bird turns its face away and half-crouches. A running bird stops so abruptly that an observer's eye keeps traveling, then has a difficult time respotting the bird as it stands motionless.

Snowy plovers are a birder's challenge, for hours of careful observation may be required to find them. Their home is the cruelest and most hostile environment in the region—alkaline flats. Here, in the absence of vegetation, temperatures reach extreme levels and life seems impossible, yet this charming and unobtrusive bird spends the summer raising its chicks in these conditions. During peak midday temperatures, the parent's sole job is cooling the eggs. Parents stand to create shade; at extreme temperatures, they also wet their breast feathers at the nearest water source and use evaporation to help cool the eggs. Once afternoon temperatures drop, parents leave the eggs unattended and search for food.

Females may turn their batch of newly hatched chicks over to the male and renest with another male; likewise, males often choose a second mate once the chicks are old enough. Chicks are quite independent, running around almost immediately after hatching, finding their own food, and walking up to 2 miles to choice feeding grounds where aquatic insects and alkali flies are abundant.

When and Where to See Them: Found almost exclusively on alkali flats from early April into September, but nest sites always located near sources of free water. May appear on muddy shorelines of other freshwater and alkaline bodies of water during migration. Uncommon except at localized breeding sites.

Snowy plovers are more visible when away from alkaline flats.

Female plover protects eggs on her simple nest.

BLACK-NECKED STILT

Himantopus mexicanus

(Gk *himantos,* a leather strap; Gk *pous,* foot. NL *mexicanus,* of Mexico)

Eye-catchers: This black-and-white shorebird with coral red legs is unmistakable. Females are dark brown, and males are jet black.

Natural History: Dainty and strikingly leggy, the black-necked stilt is an anomaly in a harsh desert landscape. The black-necked stilt is a tropical marsh bird of South and Central America that ranges north into the Great Basin. In the Great Basin, it finds companionship with its close cousin, the American avocet. The two species typically nest together, though stilts prefer to feed in marshes while avocets frequent mudflats. A straight bill, lacking the upward curve of an avocet's bill, identifies the stilt. Watch carefully as the two species feed together; note how the stilt uses its bill to pick food off the water surface, while the avocet sweeps its bill across mud surfaces like a scythe. The long legs of a stilt allow it to find its own feeding sites by wading into deeper water than other shorebirds.

Stilts and flamingos have the longest legs, relative to body size, of any bird; the distance between heel and toe in the black-necked stilt is greater than its body length. (The heels of birds form the flex point we see them bending as they walk; hence birds walk on tiptoe, the stretch between heel and toe forming the "leg.") During display flights, black-necked stilts prominently dangle their brilliantly colored legs, suggesting that their legs act as visual cues, at least during the breeding season. Their legs also act as springs to help them become airborne. These noticeable birds use their vivid colors and aggressive displays to distract predators away from their well-hidden eggs.

When and Where to See Them: Found on marshes and shallow bodies of water from late March through August. Locally common, with higher numbers in the eastern Great Basin. During drought years, breeding birds push northward in search of nesting areas, sometimes roaming as far north as Canada.

The backward-bending "knee" is the bird's heel.

The female black-necked stilt shows a brownish back.

Male stilt rests on one leg.

AMERICAN AVOCET
Recurvirostra americana
(L *recurvo,* to curve back; L *rostrum,* a bill. NL *americana,*
of America)

Eye-catchers: A large shorebird, conspicuous by its colorful plumage and by its loud protesting. The long, upturned bill and striking black-and-white pattern is further accented during the breeding season by a bright orange hood. In winter, the orange hood changes back to pale gray.

Natural History: On the bleakest, most sun-drenched, reeking shallow puddles of alkaline water, one finds the showy and graceful American avocet holding court. These areas are among the richest habitats in the Great Basin for invertebrates, so those few birds that can tolerate the alkali salts are rewarded with abundant food. On nesting grounds around alkaline waters, avocets noisily defend their eggs and chicks. They throw themselves energetically toward an intruder or flail on the ground as if mortally wounded to create a distraction.

The bill of this bird has generated much discussion because it looks so unwieldy. Avocets are actually versatile feeders, using their bills as precisely as a surgeon would forceps. In their most common feeding technique, avocets lean forward until the bill brushes the surface of the mud and then step forward at a half run, sweeping the bill from side to side like a scythe. The avocet then consumes its harvest of small invertebrates without pause. Unlike other shorebirds, avocets readily swim, and while feeding may tip bottom up in deeper water like a dabbling duck. Avocets can even dive underwater.

If you see a pair standing together, look closely at their bills—the male's bill is longer and straighter than the female's.

When and Where to See Them: Widespread throughout the western United States, but reaches its greatest concentration in the Great Basin, especially during migration. Twenty thousand at a time can be seen at Carson Lake outside Fallon, Nevada, in late April and again in mid-August. While nesting, can be common at nearly any shallow pond, but prefers alkaline waters where food is abundant. A few may winter in areas where shallow waters remain unfrozen.

American avocet in breeding plumage   *Note this male's winter plumage and long, straightish bill.*

Female on nest shows a strong up-curved bill. Inset: Young avocets are all leg.

An adult's broken-wing display and vivid markings draw an intruder's attention away from the nest.

WILLET
Catoptrophorus semipalmatus
(Gk *katoptron*, mirror; Gk *phoreus*, a bearer, referring to flashing white patch in wings. L *semi*, half; L *palma*, palm of hand, referring to partly webbed feet)

Eye-catchers: Slightly smaller than a crow, the willet appears drab gray until its wings spread to reveal a conspicuous black-and-white pattern. Its bill is stout and straight, blue gray in coloration, as are its legs. Summer breeding plumage appears boldly speckled or barred at close range. In nonbreeding plumage (rarely seen in Great Basin) willets appear uniform gray.

Natural History: For a few months each summer, marsh edges and wet meadows in the Great Basin come alive with willets. Like many other grassland species that lack elevated perches from which to sing, willets have evolved vocally and visually conspicuous courtship displays. In these displays, the wing patches are prominent as males spread their wings and vibrate them to draw attention. The loud, ringing *pill-will-willet* calls that give the bird its name accompany this display.

Arriving in April, female willets quickly set about nesting amid the commotion of displaying males. Nests are a simple scrape on the ground where willets lay four eggs. As soon as one or two eggs hatch, the parents abandon the remaining eggs to tend the chick(s). This care is brief, for the parents soon leave their flightless chicks behind and gather in premigratory staging areas. Almost as quickly, adults migrate to nonbreeding grounds on the Pacific coast, and the young follow when they can.

Young willets do not breed until they are two years old. Adults show a strong fidelity to their mates and their territories year after year. Willets may also establish temporary territories while wintering on the coastal beaches of southern California and western Mexico.

When and Where to See Them: Found around marshes, wet meadows, and flooded pastures from mid-April into June. Large numbers begin to gather in July and August, especially at large alkaline lakes, but quickly migrate south, with few remaining into September.

Willet staunchly defending its territory

After the breeding season, willets lose their barred pattern.

The willet's breeding flight showcases bold wing markings.

LONG-BILLED CURLEW
Numenius americanus
(Gk *noumenios,* happening during a new moon, referring to
the bird's sickle-shaped bill, also to a kind of curlew.
NL *americanus,* of America)

Eye-catchers: The long, down-curved bill on this large shorebird is
hard to miss, but the loud *cur-lee* calls draw even more attention. A pale
cinnamon wash on the body and wings characterizes this species.

Natural History: Once a common bird of pristine Midwestern prairies,
the long-billed curlew is now almost extirpated from this portion of its
range, but it still holds on in wet meadows such as those scattered across
the Great Basin. While most local populations only number in the dozens
per site, the Great Basin supports some of the most significant nesting
areas left for this species. Malheur National Wildlife Refuge in south-
eastern Oregon is one such site, with fifteen hundred nesting curlews.
Where original prairie habitats have been lost, long-billed curlews may
adapt to nesting in grainfields and pastures.

As a nesting bird of wet meadows, long-billed curlews arrive early
in spring to utilize these habitats before they dry up for the summer. An
extended period of noisy calling, vigorous scuffling, and spectacular roller-
coaster courtship flights mark their arrival. After the breeding season,
this species becomes inconspicuous, and soon afterward most curlews
migrate south to coastal regions in southern California and western
Mexico.

Females are noticeably larger than males, with much longer bills.
You may not see this distinction unless members of a pair are together.
The female's longer bill allows her to probe deeper and reach farther for
food than the male. The diet of the long-billed curlew includes insects,
worms, berries, and the eggs and nestlings of other birds.

When and Where to See Them: Breeds in areas with wet meadows;
arrives in late March and departs during August. Numbers vary from site
to site, but found primarily in the northern half of the Great Basin, with
good populations along the Humboldt River and its tributaries.

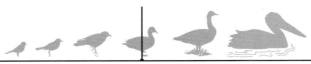

Long-billed curlews typically inhabit grasslands.

CALIFORNIA GULL
Larus californicus
(Gk *laros,* a ravenous seabird, a gull. NL *californicus,* of California)

Eye-catchers: From close range, the most distinctive marks on an adult bird are the paired red and black spots on the lower bill. Breeding adults develop brilliant red skin around their eyes and at the corners of their mouths. Juveniles, and adults at a distance, are difficult to identify. **Ring-billed gulls,** which have a black ring around the tip of their bills, also dwell in the Great Basin at many of the same sites as California gulls.

Natural History: Gulls can be common to abundant at scattered, and sometimes surprising, locations. Groups of gulls may suddenly materialize around a farmer plowing his fields, or around you just as you settle down for an idyllic picnic in a park. Flocks frequent the shores of reservoirs and lakes, while nesting adults seek out remote islands surrounded by deep water. A substantial portion of the world's California gulls breed in the Great Basin, with large colonies at Pyramid Lake, Mono Lake, and Great Salt Lake.

Leaving their coastal wintering grounds in March and April, California gulls pass over the high, snowy peaks of the Sierra Nevada, headed for Great Basin nesting sites. With loud shrieking and squabbling, nesting birds carve out tiny territories that span the distance a sitting bird can reach with its bill. Adults rigorously protect their nest against other gulls because a moment's lapse would allow their neighbors to destroy the eggs. The entire colony cooperates, however, to fiercely set upon any potential predator.

Soon after hatching, chicks become active and relatively independent, increasingly straying from the nest. By July, both adults and young birds strike out, many heading directly for ocean shores, others remaining in the interior West for several months. Gulls are notoriously opportunistic feeders, congregating wherever there is food and eating anything that appears edible.

When and Where to See Them: Primarily a summer bird in the Great Basin, though remains during winter in much reduced numbers. Most commonly observed around water, but also at city parks, campgrounds, dumps, agricultural fields, or overhead in flight.

Adult California gull in breeding plumage

Winter California gulls develop dusky markings on the head.

FORSTER'S TERN
Sterna forsteri

(OE *stern,* a tern. Name commemorates John Forster, a German naturalist who accompanied Captain James Cook on his voyage around the world in 1772)

Eye-catchers: A slight, graceful, and buoyant flier with long, narrow wings, long, deeply forked tail, a black cap, and a red bill. The **black tern,** also small and graceful, is common at many northern Great Basin marshes. The **Caspian tern** also inhabits the Great Basin, but it is stocky, larger, has a thicker bill, and lacks the deep fork in its tail.

Natural History: Forster's terns are dainty, gull-like birds, frequently observed as they swoop back and forth across open shallow waters in the Great Basin. Once you learn their distinctive, rasping, *tzaap* call, they are easier to find, for otherwise their light coloration and fast movement often make them difficult to see.

These flying habits—working back and forth, sometimes hovering—allow the Forster's tern to scan the air and water surface for insects and small fish. The bird captures its prey with spectacular headfirst dives into the water or by arcing flights across the water's surface. Forster's terns fly with their heads and bills angled downward as they scan the water below; black terns eat mainly insects and do not dive in pursuit of fish.

Forster's terns nest in loose colonies, building elaborate, well-constructed nests on floating mats formed of old bulrushes or cattails. This strategy keeps the clutches of three to four eggs dry. In the absence of these mats, pairs may construct level spots on top of muskrat houses or take over grebe nests. Young birds can swim and run at an early age; this, together with their parents' aggressive behavior, protects them from predators.

Unlike gulls, terns seldom soar while in flight, pumping their wings with a stiff jerky motion instead. Like gulls, they have webbed feet, but they do not swim much because their feet are small and weak.

When and Where to See Them: Arrives in mid- to late April, and while migrating can appear almost anywhere in the region. Stays fairly late in the fall after summering along many of the larger rivers, lakes, and marshes of the Great Basin.

Breeding Forster's tern. Inset: After breeding season, the Forster's tern's black cap becomes a black eye patch.

Caspian tern in winter. Inset: Breeding Caspian tern in flight

Black tern in winter. Inset: Breeding black tern in flight

SHORT-EARED OWL
Asio flammeus
(L *asio*, a kind of horned owl. L *flammeus*, flame-colored)

Eye-catchers: Recognize this crow-size owl by its buoyant, mothlike flight. It is often observed hunting over open grasslands and marshy areas during daylight hours. Black mask and short ear tufts distinguish it from the long-eared owl (see photo of long-eared owl on page 83).

Natural History: This ground-loving owl is a nomad, wandering far and wide in search of its favorite foods—voles and small rodents. Short-eared owls take up residence wherever prey is abundant, even staying to nest if the pickings seem especially good. Much of this wandering takes place in winter, a time when the Great Basin sees a major influx as deep snows at northern sites send short-eared owls southward.

In March and April, males engage in spectacular territorial and courtship flights, spiraling high above their territories while clapping their wings together under their bodies. During the nesting period, females remain hidden on the ground, fed by their mates. Ground-nesting birds must take special precautions to protect their nests from predators. Short-eared owls can be aggressive at the nest site, which is sometimes located on a small island. Nestlings have soft, high-pitched, begging calls that only the parents can locate. By twelve days of age the young chicks scamper away from the nest and take up residence in dense, surrounding grasses, where the parents feed them by dropping food from the air.

Short-eared owls provide a valuable service in agricultural areas because they feed so heavily on voles and other small mammals. Agricultural activities may adversely affect them, however, when equipment is used in nesting areas or when water diversions drain marshy areas. Their population appears to be in decline overall, though their nomadic nature makes accurate counts difficult.

When and Where to See Them: Found year-round in the Great Basin. In winter, numbers drop at northern sites like Malheur National Wildlife Refuge while increasing at central sites like Stillwater National Wildlife Refuge. In southern areas, rare to absent in summer but uncommon in winter. Nearly always seen in open grassy or marshy areas.

Short-eared owls stay hidden unless hunting.

Short-eared owl

Short-eared owls typically hunt over wet areas.

HOUSE WREN
Troglodytes aedon

(Gk *trogle,* hole; Gk *dytes,* diver. Gk *aedon,* a songstress, from a Greek myth of a queen who is turned into a nightingale)

Eye-catchers: The house wren is a small buffy gray bird with a cocked tail. Its body and wings are finely barred throughout. The similar **Bewick's wren** has a clear white eyebrow and appears darker overall.

Natural History: There is no experience quite like being fiercely scolded by a bird so small a whole family could fit on the palm of your hand. You do not know whether to be concerned or amused, but before you have time to decide, the bird has moved on. Darting in and out of tangled thickets with its tail cocked, bubbling over in cascading song, and wrestling with oversize nesting material, this bird is a bundle of energy. Upon returning to his nesting territory from the previous year, the male immediately sets to work building several large sample nests that he uses to woo potential mates. Females respond to a male's loud song and signal their acceptance of his work by putting the finishing touches on one of his sample nests. A male may end up with several females nesting on his territory.

In the Great Basin, the house wren's distribution is tied to the presence of trees and dense brush. Trees provide nesting sites, usually in old woodpecker holes, and brush offers secure places to search for insects. These habitats exist almost exclusively along streams, often in the mountains, and range from cottonwood or willow stands to aspen groves. Nesting cavities can be a scarce resource, and the house wren may be extremely aggressive in ousting potential competitors. Once secured, the nest hole is stuffed to capacity with sticks and feathers, shed snake skins being a favorite addition. A pair may seek out the nests of neighboring birds and kill those eggs and nestlings, potentially reducing the likelihood of attracting a nest predator, such as a fox or weasel, to the area.

When and Where to See Them: Common throughout the Great Basin, May through August, but lives year-round at southern sites. Found in the vicinity of trees with a brushy understory; breeds commonly in aspen groves and in riparian forests with numerous old or dead trees.

House wren at its nest hole.
Note its indistinct eyebrow.

Bewick's wren

MARSH WREN
Cistothorus palustris
(Gk *kistos*, a shrub; Gk *thouros*, rushing, furious.
L *palustris*, marshy)

Eye-catchers: The marsh wren is a small bird of dense marsh vegetation, heard far more often than observed. It has a short, cocked tail, a streaky back, and a white eye line.

Natural History: Marsh wrens provide the characteristic sound of any marsh with dense, emergent plants like cattails or bulrushes. Even at night or on a cold winter day males sing, but during the breeding season, marshes are a cacophony of chattering, sputtering, and loud clicking. This tireless little firebrand sings from one hundred to two hundred different songs, but to the human ear it may all sound like fierce scolding. Indeed, marsh wrens are unusually aggressive birds. They puncture eggs and kill nestlings in nests they find, whether of their own species or another; this instinct is so strong that the male will even kill his own offspring if the female leaves her nest unattended. Females raid each other's nests and immediately attack other wrens near their nest to protect their own young. Blackbirds recognize marsh wrens as an enemy and will chase one if they see it, but often the two avoid each other by nesting in different sections of a marsh.

Marsh wrens are secretive yet almost continually vocal creatures. Males may be seen popping up into the air and singing as they settle back into dense cover, but otherwise these birds stay hidden. The male builds multiple coconut-size nests, each with a distinctive hole in the side, and a large collection of nests is part of how he attracts females to his territory. He escorts a prospective mate to his collection, and she signals her acceptance by picking a nest and lining it with fine, soft materials. Successful males then build a new collection of nests to attract additional mates.

When and Where to See Them: Found at marshy sites where cattails or bulrushes grow in dense patches. Abundant throughout the Great Basin from March to November. Small populations of marsh wrens may overwinter at waters that remain unfrozen, such as thermal springs.

Male marsh wren proclaims his territory.

YELLOW WARBLER
Dendroica petechia
(Gk *dendron*, tree; Gk *oikeo*, to inhabit. E *petechiae*, a medical term for a reddish rash, from L)

Eye-catchers: The yellowest of the warblers, males are a bright, rich yellow while females are pale with a greenish tinge. Males have reddish streaks on their breast that give them their scientific name.

Natural History: When spring returns to the Great Basin, the arrival of colorful warblers is not far behind. Few are as conspicuous as the male yellow warbler singing his fast, clear *sweet sweet sweet I'm so sweet* song from the tops of willows and cottonwoods. While males sing and feed from high, exposed perches, females stay low and hidden close to their nests. Yellow warbler nests are tightly woven with a lining of pale plant down and remain intact for several years, making them a common sight when leaves fall in winter. A common parasitic pest, the brown-headed cowbird frequently chooses yellow warbler nests to lay its eggs in. When cowbird chicks hatch they displace the warbler eggs and are raised by the adult warblers. Large numbers of cowbirds in an area may eventually overwhelm a breeding population of yellow warblers. Fortunately, some warblers recognize the alien eggs, rebuild a new nest over their old one, and lay a new set of eggs. The impact of habitat loss and cowbird parasitism has elevated concerns for the future of yellow warblers, though they are still common in the Great Basin.

Researchers have extensively studied yellow warbler songs, and it appears that males use two types of songs. One form is highly variable and individualistic, allowing males to recognize each other during territorial confrontations. The other is formulaic and sung identically by all males so that females immediately recognize them as yellow warblers. During the period of active territorial defense, males also engage in special types of flight including glides with wings and tail spread, and slow flights with rapidly beating wings. Once the eggs are laid, this activity dies down and males forage low and closer to their nests.

When and Where to See Them: Found in the Great Basin from early May to the end of August. Nests in willow and cottonwood riparian zones, both on valley floors and along small creeks on mountain slopes as high as 9,000 feet. In migration, can be found temporarily in other habitats.

Female yellow warbler

Male yellow warbler

COMMON YELLOWTHROAT
Geothlypis trichas
(Gk *ge*, the earth; Gk *thlypis*, a kind of finch. Gk *trichas*, a thrush)

Eye-catchers: The common yellowthroat is an active, secretive warbler of marshes, with olive green upperparts and bright yellow underparts. Males have a wide, black mask; females have a long, rounded tail and whitish eye ring.

Natural History: Abundant and widespread in North America, the common yellowthroat is the only member of a primarily Central American genus to roam north of the Mexican border. Perhaps because it wanders so far from its ancestral home, its annual summer visit to the Great Basin is short. Arriving in May, individuals quickly breed and begin returning south by late July. During the short breeding season they are vocal and busy occupants of virtually every wet or damp area having dense tangles of vegetation. They are considered one of the most abundant warblers, though their secretive habits make it difficult to appreciate their true numbers. Singing males present the best opportunity to observe this beautiful bird. Their loud, rollicky song is *witchity witchity witchity*, and they have a distinct, dry *chack!* call.

Common yellowthroats restrict their activities to dense, low vegetation over or near water. Here they feed, nest, and raise two broods each summer. Nests are built on or near the ground and, though numerous, are rarely seen by human observers. Young birds remain dependent on their parents longer than is typical for most warblers, and the parents feed the young of the second brood right up to the time of migration. Their diet consists of insects and spiders picked from the ground and from leaf surfaces. In the month of August, common yellowthroats seem particularly abundant as young birds join adults preparing to migrate.

When and Where to See Them: Very common in marshes and wet thickets from May to mid-September; many begin heading south by late July.

Male common yellowthroat

Female yellowthroat shows less yellow than the female yellow warbler.

YELLOW-BREASTED CHAT
Icteria virens
(Gk *ikteros,* jaundice, hence yellowness. L *virens,* green)

Eye-catchers: The yellow-breasted chat is a large, beautiful warbler, with grayish olive upperparts and deep yellow underparts. Note its thick, unwarbler-like bill and long, rounded tail.

Natural History: Dense streamside thickets are the favored haunts of the yellow-breasted chat, a noisy yet secretive bird that is best described as a clownish ventriloquist. Visit these thickets and you may be serenaded by a dazzling vocal onslaught, yet find the singer invisible. The chat's behavior teases intruders as it moves ahead just out of sight, then falls silent, circling around behind with a burst of new calls.

The song itself is loud and complex; P. A. Taverner, an early Canadian ornithologist, wrote that the male yellow-breasted chat "laughs dryly, gurgles derisively, whistles triumphantly, chatters provokingly, and chuckles complacently, all in one breath." During the full moon or partially full moons the chat may sing most of the night. Male chats are most visible in early morning, when they sing from high perches; later in the day they remain in the deep interior of impenetrable thickets. Males may also be conspicuous when they perform flight songs during courtship. Rising up into the air with legs dangling freely, a male sings with his head raised and tail waving, hovers briefly, then drops back down and out of sight.

The yellow-breasted chat differs from its warbler cousins, and early biologists grouped it with various bird families before deciding that it was a warbler—a fact later confirmed using DNA analysis. Its thick bill is unique among the warblers, but, like other warblers, the yellow-breasted chat possesses nine primary flight feathers and a deeply cleft inner toe.

When and Where to See Them: Formerly widespread or even common in riparian habitats across the Great Basin but now declining, especially in areas where native willows and buffaloberries are replaced by Russian olives. Adversely affected by large-scale herbicide applications to eradicate willows, but have returned to areas recovering from this treatment. Present in the Great Basin from May to September.

Yellow-breasted chats generally stay within the interior of dense shrubs.

Male yellow-breasted chats ascend to high branches to sing.

SONG SPARROW
Melospiza melodia

(Gk *melos*, song; Gk *spiza*, finch. L *melodia*, a pleasant song)

Eye-catchers: The song sparrow is a richly streaked, brown and gray sparrow of marshes and wet areas. At least three subspecies inhabit the Great Basin, all slightly different in appearance but all showing a dark central spot on the breast. Look for its weak, jerky flight, in which the tail is pumped up and down.

Natural History: Song sparrows are the most variable, and one of the best studied, birds in North America. Although they are a common and familiar bird in the Great Basin, their distribution is limited to areas with water. Whether along streams, in wet meadows, or around marshes, song sparrows stay close to low, dense vegetation, darting in and out of dark thickets where their streaky coloration blends in perfectly with the mosaic of shadows.

During the breeding season, males conspicuously ascend to high elevated perches to sing loudly. Once mated, however, they become quiet and secretive to protect the presence of their well-hidden nests. The female performs most of the nesting duties until her chicks leave the nest, whereupon the male takes charge of them and she begins a second, and sometimes a third and a fourth, clutch of eggs.

Pairs may stay together in successive years, and if they migrate, most return to their territory from the previous year. Research shows that some individuals migrate while others stay through the winter, and an individual who migrates one year may not do so in subsequent years. While it may appear that song sparrows are present year-round, summer breeding birds frequently head south and are replaced in winter by northern subspecies. You can detect this changeover if you look closely at minute details in the coloration of song sparrows through the seasons.

When and Where to See Them: Year-round in low valleys and foothills where dense vegetation and water occur together. Song sparrows in the Great Basin are a mix of summer-only birds, migrants, winter visitors, and permanent residents. Periods of peak movement are in March, September, and October.

Perched on a cattail, a song sparrow brings food to its nest.

RED-WINGED BLACKBIRD
Agelaius phoeniceus
(Gk *agelaios,* flocking or gregarious, from *agele,* a herd.
Gk *phoinikos,* crimson)

Eye-catchers: One of several species of blackbirds, but the male's brilliant red shoulder patches easily identify it. In winter other feathers can cover the red patch, however. Females show tinges of peach or red in their heavily streaked plumage.

Natural History: What a transformation in February, when flocks of grubby, black feedlot birds move to marshes and begin singing a loud, ringing *conk-a-ree!* When their black feathers shine with reflected sunlight and the males fluff out their jewel-like shoulder epaulets, they hardly seem the same birds. This behavior shows the power of the color red in the animal kingdom, for males uncover their red patches when they want to signal aggressive territorial intent. Research shows that males whose red feathers are experimentally covered cannot defend their territories against other males.

After giving the males a few weeks to sort things out, the females arrive and select males with the best territories as mates. As many as nine females will nest in close proximity to protect each other's eggs and nestlings from predation by marsh wrens. Other enemies and competitors include northern harriers, whose very appearance can send a marsh full of blackbirds into an uproar, and yellow-headed blackbirds, a larger and closely related enemy who drives red-wings out of prime marsh sites.

Red-winged blackbirds cluster in winter flocks of thousands of birds (hence the reference to a herd in their scientific name). Although at times these numbers damage crops, they also consume tons of harmful insects and grubs.

When and Where to See Them: Congregate in large groups all winter in lower valleys and agricultural areas. Move to marshes, wet meadows, and riparian areas in the spring. Common in valley wetlands, but breed upward to mountain meadows and streamside corridors. Part of the population appears to migrate south in September, returning early in February before most other migrants.

Female red-winged blackbird

Male red-winged blackbirds fluff out their red shoulders when displaying. Inset: Singing male red-winged blackbird

Mixed flock of red-winged and yellow-headed blackbirds in winter

YELLOW-HEADED BLACKBIRD
Xanthocephalus xanthocephalus
(Gk *xanthos,* yellow; Gk *cephalos,* head)

Eye-catchers: All individuals show some degree of yellow about the head and breast, ranging from a full brilliant hood in males to a reduced bib in females. Winter birds develop dusky mottling that partly obscures the yellow. Males also show a distinct white wing patch.

Natural History: Yellow-headed blackbirds dominate the smaller red-winged blackbirds at marshes and take first choice of prime nesting habitats. Ironically, this choice seems to have evolved into a limitation, for yellow-headed blackbirds now depend on sites with tall, emergent vegetation over standing water. If the water dries up at any point, they abandon the colony and their nests. Red-wings, used to being pushed into marginal habitats, are instead flexible. The narrow habitat requirements of yellow-headed blackbirds show up readily in large marshes, for rather than forming one large colony they more often nest in small scattered groups corresponding to perfect site conditions.

It seems one of the great injustices of the avian world that such a marvelously plumaged bird should be burdened with the most grating voice. Courting males do their very best but merely manage a simple, raspy bellow. If nothing else, it is a loud call, designed to attract females to the sometimes isolated and scattered breeding grounds. This grating voice is another irony of the yellow-headed blackbird's dominance over its sweet-voiced cousin, the red-wing.

While their males vocalize above, females stay low in dense cattails, seemingly nonchalant about the territorial boundaries of males but vigorously defending the space around their own nests. They carefully construct their nests from wet aquatic weeds that dry and tighten into secure structures woven between standing stems. The female may build several nests before settling on one, even though the nestlings don't stay around long and "jump ship" just a week after hatching.

When and Where to See Them: Flocks may remain through winter, but mainly a summer bird. Can be observed during the breeding season perching on cattails or feeding on the muddy margins of ponds. Following breeding, males flock separately from females with juveniles. Feeds on grains, seeds, and insects in grassy areas. Shows up throughout the region during migration.

Male yellow-headed blackbird

Male in winter plumage

Female yellow-headed blackbird

BULLOCK'S ORIOLE
Icterus bullockii
(Gk *ikteros,* jaundice, hence yellow, also a name for a yellow green bird. Commemorates William Bullock, an English traveler of the early 1800s who collected the first specimen near Mexico City)

Eye-catchers: The male is brilliant, fluorescent orange and jet black; distinguish it from other orioles by its orange outer tail feathers and an orange eyebrow. Females and juveniles look like other orioles and like the female western tanager, but the whitish belly is a helpful mark.

Natural History: Truly a tropical species, the Bullock's oriole arrives late, nests quickly, and leaves early to return to Mexico and Central America. One reason it flies north is to find immense quantities of weevils and caterpillars that feed its insatiably hungry chicks. For this reason alone, the Bullock's oriole is an ally for anyone growing cultivated plants. Orioles readily adapt to humans and are quite common about ranches, city parks, and residential areas, where people welcome their colorful and lively presence.

Bullock's orioles select groves of tall, deciduous trees in which to nest. At one time this habitat was limited to river corridors in desert valleys and on lower mountain slopes, but trees planted around houses and ranches have enabled this attractive bird to expand its range. When leaves drop in autumn, the nests of this common bird are conspicuous. Woven from pale plant fibers, fishing line, horsehair, and string, the pouchlike hanging nest of the oriole is one of the most familiar bird nests in the Great Basin. At some sites, limited habitat forces several to nest close together, giving the false appearance that this species is a colonial nester.

Females lack the brilliant colors of males, though they share the ability to sing loud, somewhat musical songs. The ability to sing may help a female acquire a new mate if she loses the first one early in the breeding season.

When and Where to See Them: Arrives early in May and nests in tall, deciduous trees at lower elevations, mostly near streams or human habitations. Found in a wider variety of habitats while migrating, with most leaving the Great Basin by the end of August.

Female Bullock's oriole

Male Bullock's oriole

Sagebrush-rabbitbrush habitat in Great Basin

Pueblo Mountains, Oregon

Sage steppe, Malheur National Wildlife Refuge, Oregon

BIRDS OF DESERTS
AND OPEN COUNTRY

Deserts and open country include everything that is dry, but not a mountain, in the Great Basin. At first glance, the desert appears monotonous and uniform, but it actually comprises many habitat types. Among the most conspicuous are sagebrush, shadscale, and greasewood plant communities. Because water is limited, birds of this zone travel regularly to water sources or obtain water from the food they eat.

TURKEY VULTURE
Cathartes aura

(Gk *kathartes,* a purifier. Origin of *aura* uncertain, likely a Latinized version of a South American name for this bird)

Eye-catchers: Identify this large, hawklike bird by its unsteady, rocking flight and by its wings, held upward in a V. The red, featherless head of the adult bird may appear black at a distance. The juvenile's head is gray.

Natural History: No desert scene is complete without vultures, and the Great Basin is no exception. Turkey vultures are a common sight—large, dark, ominous birds circling in the sky or perched beside roadside carrion. Turkey vultures are soaring specialists and spend nearly all their time aloft, soaring for hours without a single wing beat. They have become so specialized at soaring that their poorly developed breast muscles (which power the wings) make flight, especially takeoff, ungainly and labored. Turkey vultures are also specialists at conserving energy, and in the morning they perch in the sunlight with wings spread, soaking up the sun's warmth rather than using fat supplies to generate their own heat.

Hot days provide perfect conditions for soaring because columns of rapidly rising air, called thermals, form as the ground heats up each day. To stay aloft, a soaring bird maintains momentum by falling forward in a constant downward glide. Thermals carry the falling bird upward faster than it sinks, so the overall effect is flight. Vultures do not move much on cold days and leave the region during winter.

Turkey vultures lay their eggs in shallow caves or on secluded canyon walls, often in the mountains. From these sites, adults fan out each day into lower valleys, where they have a better chance of finding thermals and the large dead animals they feed on. Dispersed over large areas, circling vultures watch both the ground and each other. When one descends to feed, its sharp-eyed neighbors hurry over to join the feast.

Scientists once classified vultures with raptors but now consider them to be closely related to storks, ibis, and herons.

When and Where to See Them: Common and widespread from March to October; most frequently observed in valleys and over lower mountain slopes. When not breeding, up to two hundred will gather to sleep at traditional roosts, typically in groves of large trees.

Turkey vulture in flight shows long feathers at tips of wing.

Turkey vultures roost communally at night. Inset: Lack of feathers around the face helps keep vultures clean when feeding on carrion.

Turkey vultures start the day soaking up the sun's warmth.

RED-TAILED HAWK
Buteo jamaicensis
(L *buteo,* a hawk. NL *jamaicensis,* of Jamaica, referring to site of first specimen)

Eye-catchers: This highly variable hawk can range from rich, dark brown to extremely pale, though most are mottled brown and white. When seen in good light the adult's red tail is diagnostic. Other field marks include the combination of a dark throat, a light chest, and a dark belly band. In flight, look for the dark, comma-shaped mark at the bend in the wing, and for the dark bar at the front edge of the wing near the neck. Young birds lack the red tail but show the other marks.

Natural History: Red-tailed hawks, like all soaring hawks known as buteos, have broad wings and tails to help catch and ride subtle air currents. This design strategy is different from falcons, another familiar family of raptors, whose long, narrow wings are designed for swift, powerful flight.

From high in the air, red-tails circle and scan for small mammals and birds that they capture by diving and chasing. Small birds, particularly blackbirds, also mob and chase red-tails and other large hawks that they see as a threat. One reason why hawks spend so much time aloft may be to avoid the mobbing blackbirds, which can be as pesky as a swarm of mosquitoes.

In early spring, red-tails begin elaborate courtship displays by swooping at their mates with legs dangling. The female, larger than her mate, frequently rolls onto her back and locks talons with the male while in flight. These displays are accompanied by loud piercing screams, *kee-eer,* the archetypal hawk call used in movie soundtracks. Soon after courtship, the pair constructs a large, bulky nest in a tall tree or cliff face. If possible, the pair reuses this nest in subsequent years, but nesting great horned owls (who do not build their own nests) often claim it first.

When and Where to See Them: Very common permanent resident. Numbers decline in summer, as many move north to breed, and territory defense spreads out the ones that remain in the Great Basin. Found at any elevation most of the year but concentrates around snow-free valleys and ranches in winter.

A light juvenile

Typical adult red-tailed hawk with red tail

A dark juvenile

Note the wing markings in flight.

ROUGH-LEGGED HAWK
Buteo lagopus

(L *buteo,* a hawk. Gk *lagos,* a hare; Gk *pous,* foot; referring to feathered feet)

Eye-catchers: This dark and mottled bird has a pale head and a white tail with a wide black band at the tip, which is diagnostic in flight. The lower belly ranges from heavily streaked to black banded.

Natural History: This large, dark hawk of the arctic tundra roams south in winter to avoid deep snows and bitter cold. Many rough-legged hawks winter in the Great Basin, but actual numbers vary from year to year depending on weather. In the Great Basin, as in their summer home of the north, they inhabit open country, including agricultural areas, and grasslands. Here they watch from low perches or the ground, waiting to catch their favorite foods, mice and voles. They are one of the few hawks that also hunt by hovering in midair. Hovering takes place 50 to 100 feet above the ground and functions to keep the bird stationary while allowing it to pinpoint a furtive prey item below.

Unlike many other hawks, the rough-legged hawk has feathering down its legs to its feet. This feature, giving the bird its common and scientific names, is an adaptation to arctic cold, since much of a bird's heat is lost from its bare legs and feet. In Asia, some authors have called this same species the shaggy-legged buzzard.

Since rough-legged hawks probably mate for life, it is likely that pairs winter in close proximity to each other, and observers have noted that some recognizable individuals return each year to the same wintering sites. During winter months these hawks roost communally at night and disperse at daybreak to favored hunting spots.

When and Where to See Them: First arrives in October, becoming common to abundant by November. Numbers are much higher in the northern Great Basin. Common about agricultural areas and wetlands in valleys. Highest numbers in North America recorded for several winters at Malheur National Wildlife Refuge. Slow return to the arctic in March and April, following the melting snow.

Rough-legged hawk

Rough-legged hawk in flight

AMERICAN KESTREL
Falco sparverius
(LL *falco* derives from L *falx,* sickle, for shape of talons and bill. L *sparverius,* pertaining to a sparrow)

Eye-catchers: This small, fast, agile falcon hovers on rapidly beating wings. When perched, it may bob its tail and pump its head nervously. At close range, look for the paired dark sideburns on its face. Both sexes have reddish tails, but females have uniformly brown upperparts and males show blue gray wings.

Natural History: American kestrels are the most common summer raptor in the Great Basin, and their ready proximity to civilization makes them an ideal bird to study. Relatively heedless of human activity, they take up residence about ranches and parks with tall trees. They can be abundant along stream channels where tall old cottonwoods present tree cavities in which to nest. Fierce competition for the few available cavities forces kestrels to be flexible and tolerant; they frequently occupy nest boxes put out for their use.

A lively, vocal nature makes kestrels conspicuous. This is especially true around the nest, where males perform spectacular roller-coaster flights for the female while shrilly calling *killy killy killy.* As the female tends the nest, the male makes repeated visits to feed her large insects, small mammals, and birds. He feeds her throughout the nest-building and incubation period.

Kestrels typically hunt from perches, but because so much of their terrain is open they use hovering in midair as an alternate hunting technique. The kestrel kills its prey with a quick bite, plucking off and discarding hair, feathers, and hard parts (such as the wings and legs on insects) before consumption. Kestrels may cache surplus food for several days and eat it later.

When and Where to See Them: Widespread throughout the Great Basin wherever there are trees with cavities. Favors old cottonwoods for nesting sites but will use any available cavity if necessary. During winter, mountain populations move into valleys or leave the coldest areas entirely. A substantial number from other regions migrate across the Great Basin in spring and autumn.

Male kestrels scan for prey from high perches.

Female American kestrel

PRAIRIE FALCON
Falco mexicanus

(LL *falco* derives from L *falx,* sickle, referring to shape of claws and talons. NL *mexicanus,* of Mexico)

Eye-catchers: At close range, look for a single narrow streak below the eye on this pale brown, crow-size falcon. In flight, it shows dark "armpits." Adults have a spotted breast, while juveniles show streaks on their underparts.

Natural History: Unlike hawks, with their broad tails and wings for soaring, falcons have long, narrow, pointed wings designed for extremely fast and maneuverable flight. In full pursuit, falcons can chase down virtually any animal. Prairie falcons of the arid West are one of the fastest birds known, sometimes outpacing even the master flier, the peregrine falcon. Whereas peregrines hunt from on high, prairie falcons utilize stealth to surprise small birds and mammals on the ground. From low perches they power into lightning-fast flight at grass-top level and strike down unsuspecting prey. They grab smaller animals without even a pause in flight, and strike larger ones a debilitating blow with the falcon's clenched feet. Prairie falcons prefer such ground-loving birds as horned larks and western meadowlarks but hunt ground squirrels and rabbits as well. When males feed females on the nest they may eat the heads first and then feed their mate the headless prey.

Though birds of open country, prairie falcons seek out cliff faces adjacent to grasslands and sagebrush flats for nesting. Their typical nest site is a simple ledge with a protective overhang, but they also use old raven or hawk nests. Daily foraging runs can take them to valleys great distances from the nest in search of food.

In winter some prairie falcons head south or follow flocks of horned larks, but many simply move down to valleys and fields where large concentrations of blackbirds and starlings make for easy pickings. By the following February or March, males and females return to old nest sites, and males begin elaborate aerial courtship displays in preparation for nesting.

When and Where to See Them: Frequently seen on telephone poles and fence posts, especially in agricultural areas. Although common and widespread at all times, fall is the peak time to see them because young birds and northern migrants join the resident populations. Numbers dwindle in winter.

Falcons have narrow, pointed wings.

*Adult prairie falcon on typical perch with juvenile
(inset) showing the young bird's streaked breast*

SAGE GROUSE
Centrocercus urophasianus
(Gk *kentron*, a point, spine; Gk *kerkos*, tail. Gk *oura*, the tail; Gk *phasianos*, a pheasant)

Eye-catchers: If this large, long-tailed grouse is startled, it may erupt off the ground in a noisy explosion of lumbering flight. Its blackish belly separates it from female ring-necked pheasants, a common introduced bird.

Natural History: The male sage grouse has one of the most energetic courtship displays of any Great Basin bird. Throwing his full body into action from February till May, the male makes what could be considered either a ridiculous or a noble expression of his amatory interest. Gathered together on traditional display grounds known as leks, dozens to hundreds of male sage grouse compete for the attention of females. Females consistently mate only with the one or two most dominant males while ignoring all the other suitors who puff out their chests, fan their spiny tails, and strut around making a gurgling popping sound with air in their throats.

Sage grouse live year-round in the shelter of sagebrush, and their winter diet consists almost entirely of sagebrush leaves. This diet has several advantages: it is plentiful, easily digested, and high in protein, fat, and carbohydrates. Throughout the Great Basin, sage grouse populations are declining as humans subtly alter habitat or convert it to other uses. In particular, grazing and fire suppression encourage invasion by non-native plants and sagebrush. These choke out the forbs and grasses that provide critical food sources during the nesting season. Intensive efforts are under way to restore sage grouse populations at historically used sites.

When and Where to See Them: May be seen in wet meadows from late June to mid-October, but for guaranteed views visit a lek site in early spring. Leks are highly susceptible to disturbance so it is best to visit with an experienced guide, arrive well before sunrise, and remain in a car or a blind to avoid disturbing displaying birds. Sage grouse spend most of the year at lowland sites, except in late summer and fall when they ascend onto mountain slopes, where they can be numerous around seeps and springs. They may winter on windswept ridges up to 8,000 feet.

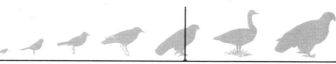

Male sage grouse goes to extremes to attract a female.

A magnificent sight

Male sage grouse

MOURNING DOVE
Zenaida macroura
(Named by Charles Bonaparte, the "father of systematic ornithology in America," to commemorate his wife, Princess Zenaide. Gk *macros*, long; Gk *oura*, tail)

Eye-catchers: The mourning dove is a sleek, streamlined, gray brown bird with a long, tapering tail and black-spotted wings. Note the small, bobbing head, and wings that whistle as the bird takes flight. In flight, it resembles the American kestrel, but the dove has a distinctively narrow pointed tail. At close range, the male shows hints of blue and green on its neck and rose pink on its breast.

Natural History: Mourning dove pairs are a picture of gentleness as they rub necks, preen each other, and *coo* softly. Perhaps Bonaparte named these birds for his wife because they reflected his own affection for her. The male's amorous courtship displays continue with energetic flights and strutting walks before the female. Their familiar mournful *oh-ah cooo-cooo coo* call is an advertisement of readiness and availability. Once paired, males become silent and diligent helpers at the nest.

A female signals her readiness to mate by visiting several potential nest sites selected by the male and preening him when she sees one she likes. The male gathers nesting material but the female constructs the nest, which can be in a tree, on a rock outcropping, or on the ground. They take turns incubating the eggs and raising the naked, helpless young.

Mourning doves do well in arid environments though their exclusive diet of dry seeds necessitates frequent visits to open water. They are strong, swift fliers and readily travel long distances to reach food and water. Unlike other birds that tilt their heads up to swallow after each sip, pigeons and doves can fulfill their water needs with one long, continuous drink. This adaptation reduces their time of exposure to predators who lurk around watering holes.

After young birds fledge, mourning doves form gregarious groups. Look for them near open fields and along roads where weed seeds accumulate.

When and Where to See Them: Found in open areas below 8,000 feet. Abundant and widespread, often associated with riparian habitats. A few overwinter, but the majority begin to arrive in late March and leave in August.

This female illustrates the small-headed appearance of mourning doves.

Male mourning dove shows hints of color.

GREAT HORNED OWL
Bubo virginianus
(L *bubo,* a great horned owl. NL *virginianus,* of Virginia)

Eye-catchers: This large, hawk-size owl with prominent "horns" has fine, dense streaking that runs horizontally across the chest and belly. The similar, but smaller, **long-eared owl** shows vertical streaking and horns that are closely set together.

Natural History: In late winter before leaves come out on large cottonwoods, look for great horned owls incubating eggs laid in old, abandoned red-tailed hawk nests. With such an early start, sometimes nesting before the snows end, great horned owl chicks are off the nest and learning to hunt in time to feed on young mammals and birds in June. Adult great horned owls do not build their own nests but use cliff ledges or nests made by ravens, hawks, or eagles. If necessary, a determined great horned owl will evict a nest's owner. Great horned owls are powerful, ferocious, and intolerant of other owls or hawks nesting nearby.

Great horned owls consume a great variety of items—anything that moves—from scorpion to adult goose. They feed heavily on rabbits, ground squirrels, and gophers; will even eat porcupines and skunks; and have been known to wade into water to capture fish. One of their greatest impacts, however, is on other birds of prey; when a great horned owl moves into a neighborhood other hawks and owls leave or get eaten. This arrangement undoubtedly reduces competition for food.

A great horned owl pair holds its territory for life (on the order of thirteen years) and rarely leaves it. Courtship begins in midwinter, is noisy, and includes ritual feeding by the male. This feeding may establish the male's ability to provide for the female, because he feeds her and the nestlings as long as she remains on the nest. He caches extra food in the nest, and the male and female continue to feed the young for more than two months.

The great horned owl of the Americas is part of a worldwide group of owls known as eagle owls, and some authorities consider it an American form of the Eurasian eagle owl.

When and Where to See Them: Common and widespread in both mountains and deserts, most often observed in groups of tall cottonwoods around water or homesteads.

Fledgling great horned owl

The long-eared owl is superficially similar to the great horned owl.

Horizontal breast streaking is visible on the great horned owl.

COMMON NIGHTHAWK
Chordeiles minor
(Gk *chorde,* a musical instrument; Gk *deile,* evening. L *minor,* smaller; incorrectly thought to be smallest nighthawk when named)

Eye-catchers: Secretive while on the ground, the common nighthawk is conspicuous and noisy when flying at dusk with loud, raspy, *spee-ick* calls, long, narrow, blackish wings with a white bar, and stiff, erratic wing beats. The smaller common poorwill, a close cousin of the nighthawk, has finely barred wings without a white patch.

Natural History: Common nighthawks are one of those odd birds that catch the attention even of nonbirdwatchers. Like giant bats, they crisscross the evening sky in darting flight. At first they flutter upward at intervals, as if climbing stairs, then they dash downward with a curious buzz made by wind rushing through their wings. All the while they catch flying insects in their broad, gaping mouths. Males direct this same swooping flight, ending in a *boom* or *buzz,* at females perched on the ground, sometimes swooping steeply downward to within a few feet of the ground. The male also strives to catch the female's attention by landing and spreading his tail while fluffing out his gleaming white throat feathers.

The female lays two eggs on the ground in that most inhospitable of places, barren open spaces with no shade. With daytime ground temperatures soaring well over one hundred degrees, she must pant heavily by fluttering her throat pouch to cool herself down.

This long-distance migrant is the last bird to arrive in the Great Basin each spring, and as soon as the young can fly they return to South America. Long, narrow wings are a trademark feature of long-distance migrants.

Common poorwills are rarely seen, though you can hear their whistled *poor-will* song on warm summer evenings throughout the Great Basin.

When and Where to See Them: Arrives in late May and early June when the weather is warm and insects abundant. Common migrant passing through the Great Basin, with large numbers remaining to breed in open areas. Populations may be in decline, particularly around metropolitan areas with large-scale pesticide programs. During the day, perches on wires, fence posts, and branches, where it sits lengthwise rather than crosswise; circles in the sky in early evening.

Common nighthawk on daytime perch

Common nighthawk sometimes shows black-and-white patch on folded wing.

Common poorwill is a rare sight.

SAY'S PHOEBE
Sayornis saya

(Gk *ornis*, bird; *Sayornis* literally means "Say's bird." Named for Thomas Say, one of America's premier naturalists in the early 1800s, who despite poor health, made two arduous treks to the Rocky Mountains)

Eye-catchers: Say's phoebe is an active, darting bird of low perches in open, arid areas. Grayish brown in color overall, with a characteristic pale orangish belly, it often dips and fans its blackish tail when perched.

Natural History: This wispy, buoyant bird may seem forlorn, both for the barren spaces it inhabits and for its plaintive *pee-ee* call. Examine further and you will find it an energetic presence, constantly flitting back and forth to catch insects.

Say's phoebes are birds of dry, open landscapes, barely tolerating scattered shrubs except as vantage points from which to scan the ground. In areas that lack shrubs they hover low over the ground or even sit on dirt clods and small rocks. Within the flycatcher family, they occupy a unique niche in catching insects that live on the ground (also see gray flycatcher on page 124). Perhaps because ground insects warm up quickly and become active early in the year, Say's phoebes are one of the first migrants to return in the spring.

While widespread as migrants, during nesting they require ledges that are protected from the midday sun by an overhang. Say's phoebes obtain all their liquid from the insects they eat, so a shady nest site helps them conserve water. Historically, Say's phoebes used canyon walls and cliffs, but they have easily adapted to the undersides of bridges, abandoned buildings, and old mine shafts. These birds are now a familiar neighbor of human habitations.

After raising their first brood early in the summer, the female quickly lays a second clutch while the male continues to feed the first group of youngsters.

When and Where to See Them: Arrives in open, dry country starting in late February; migrants widely observed through April. Nesting birds prefer rocky cliffs, abandoned buildings, and bridges from low valleys up to 7,000 feet. Most nesting and migrating birds leave by the end of September, though a few overwinter, especially in the southern end of the Great Basin.

*With a fresh catch, this Say's phoebe
shows off its belly and tail.*

*Rictal bristles around the bill
help flycatchers pinpoint prey.*

WESTERN KINGBIRD
Tyrannus verticalis
(L *tyrannus,* a tyrant. L *verticalis,* relating to the vertex or top of the head, referring to a reddish crown that is usually concealed)

Eye-catchers: An active bird of open country, the western kingbird has a yellowish belly and blackish tail with white outer margins. Its black bill is stout for catching large, hard-bodied insects.

Natural History: Probably no ranch or rural neighborhood in the open expanses of the Great Basin lacks western kingbirds. In proper neighborly fashion, kingbirds are social and communicative, twittering among themselves. They scold intruders and keep up a busy traffic chasing other birds.

Historically, western kingbirds occupied streamside areas where they nested in cottonwoods, but they have since expanded their range by nesting on telephone poles, barns, and other human structures. You often see them from the road perched on fence posts and telephone wires. These elevated perches in an otherwise flat, featureless landscape allow them to scan widely for the large flying insects that form the bulk of their diet. Young kingbirds are voracious and demand a steady supply of grass-hoppers, beetles, wasps, and bees, keeping their parents busy.

In the manner of flycatchers, kingbirds dart out from high perches and maneuver after insects with an agile, twisting flight. A set of long, rictal bristles at the base of the bill precisely guides the flycatcher's final split-second snap. As the young birds grow up, parents release injured prey for the young to practice catching. By late July, most pairs have raised their families and have headed back to their winter home in Mexico and Central America.

When and Where to See Them: Arrives in late April and May. Nests in the open country of valleys, but lives as high as 7,500 feet, so long as there is a dependable supply of insects.

The western kingbird is a larger bird than the Say's phoebe (page 86) and has a bright yellow belly with a hint of a dark mask.

LOGGERHEAD SHRIKE
Lanius ludovicianus
(L *lanius,* a butcher. NL *ludovicianus,* of Louisiana, where it was first collected)

Eye-catchers: This striking bird perches prominently on fences, wires, and exposed branches. Its black mask, wings, and tail contrast sharply with its bluish gray upperparts; a concealed white patch on its wing shows in flight. Its wing beat is a series of rapid flaps, then a glide, resulting in a deeply undulating flight.

Natural History: Like a tiny hawk, the loggerhead shrike is a fierce predator. Observe its strong, hooked bill and the way it watches from high perches, and you will see the resemblance. In fact, shrikes share with *Accipiter* hawks the short, rounded wings and long, rudderlike tail that enable fast, exceedingly agile pursuit of prey. They are one of only a few songbirds that, like hawks, regularly kill vertebrate prey.

Their lack of strong, taloned feet has led to the evolution of the shrike's most curious behavior; they impale prey on thorns and barbed wire fences to hold it in place while they tear off bite-size pieces with their bills. Sometimes this "butcher bird" impales mice, birds, lizards, or large insects, to be consumed hours or days later. Males, who feed females on the nest, impale food near the nest so the female has ready access to it whenever she is hungry.

Solitary most of the year, shrikes pair up to breed, then split apart as soon as the young are independent. Shrikes build their nests in small, dense trees or shrubs, in arid habitats with plenty of bare ground where it is easy to spot prey. Males become agitated and emit a staccato series of *bzeek* notes when an intruder enters the nesting territory. While males also sing a combination of squeaky notes and low warbles, they sing more often in fall and winter when they defend their own solitary feeding territories.

When and Where to See Them: Common throughout the region but prefers dry, open areas with scattered perching sites including fence posts, shrubs, and telephone lines. Found in valleys and foothills, though individuals may wander upslope into mountains after breeding. Numbers decline in winter, especially in cold northern areas.

The loggerhead shrike uses its hooked bill to tear apart prey.

BLACK-BILLED MAGPIE
Pica pica
(L *pica,* magpie)

Eye-catchers: The black-billed magpie is one of the Great Basin's most familiar birds. No other large bird combines a vivid black-and-white pattern with a long tail. The wings and tail are iridescent with hints of blue, green, and purple showing in bright sunlight. In flight, magpies flash a white wing patch with each wing beat.

Natural History: Like all members of the highly intelligent crow family, magpies have a good memory, learn easily, and exhibit complex behavior. They interact readily with their neighbors, whether animal or human, and become tame or fearful depending on how they are treated.

Young magpies learn about predators, food sources, and appropriate magpie social behavior by staying with their parents through late summer and fall, a longer period of time than in most other species of birds. As the seasons become colder, these family groups join into small flocks that stay together through winter. Many magpies remain near their home range year-round but there is some migratory movement, particularly of birds in northern regions.

Well before spring returns, magpies reestablish pair bonds from the previous year. Since their large, domed nests require six weeks to construct, a pair tries to locate and reuse their old one, but often small mammals or other birds have already claimed it. While the nest's thorny exterior protects the eggs and magpies from predators, a magpie in the open is vulnerable to attack by hawks. Short wings diminish their flight speed, so magpies prefer to stay close to dense shrubs into which they can dive for protection.

Magpies spend much of their time on the ground, walking about with a swagger and their long tails half-cocked, searching for grains, seeds, and grasshoppers and other insects. They also consume carrion and have learned to scan roadsides for dead animals.

When and Where to See Them: Common resident of valleys and foothills, absent in the southern end of the Great Basin. Favors open shrub lands and woodlands. Nests in dense trees and thickets near water. Numbers may decline in winter in colder regions.

Black-billed magpie

COMMON RAVEN
Corvus corax
(L *corvus,* a crow or raven. Gk *corax,* a crow or raven, *corax* may be imitative of its call)

Eye-catchers: Distinguish the common raven from the smaller American crow by its wedge-shaped tail and hoarse, croaking call. At close range, note its shaggy throat feathers and massive bill.

Natural History: Ravens are the largest of the songbirds and, while they lack the musical repertoires of their fellow songbirds, they possess a diverse vocabulary. The range of vocalizations, coupled with high degrees of intelligence and memory, gives rise to what some researchers consider a language. Whenever ravens gather together in large, social groups, which happens frequently, it is obvious that they have much to say. Their most common vocalization is a loud, croaking call that allows individuals to stay in communication over a great distance. The jet-black plumage also functions as a social signal, for the color is easy to spot and track, even across a broad desert valley.

At one time, ravens appeared to live primarily in the mountains, crossing desert valleys merely to commute to another mountain range. Telephone and power lines and poles provide ravens with a plethora of elevated perches and potential nest sites, which they readily utilize. Ravens still prefer cliffs for nesting, both for the security they offer and for updrafts upon which to soar. Pairs of ravens maintain two or more nests that they use alternately in different years, but their empty nests are sometimes used by other raptors, just as ravens will use old hawk or eagle nests.

Males feed females throughout the incubation period, often traveling long distances to secure food. Primarily scavengers, they also capture small prey if an opportunity arises. Along with vultures, ravens provide a useful service by disposing of carrion, especially along roads. Unfortunately, they are also efficient, destructive egg predators in marshes.

When and Where to See Them: Commonly observed throughout the Great Basin, often along roads where they find dead animals, and about cliffs where they nest. In late summer, some wander to higher elevations before descending to valleys, where they concentrate in winter.

The wedge-shaped tail is distinctive in flight.

Common raven's bill looks oversize.

HORNED LARK
Eremophila alpestris

(Gk *eremos,* solitary, uninhabited; Gk *philos,* loving, may be translated as desert loving. NL *alpestris,* of the Alps, alpine)

Eye-catchers: This bird appears a uniform sandy brown until it turns to face you and shows off a yellow face and black mask. Males also display a pair of black horns. In flight, look for a low, undulating flight pattern and a blackish tail, which flashes white on the outer edges.

Natural History: This "desert-loving" bird would be more accurately described as a ground lover: it spends its life on barren wastes, empty fields, and exposed soils. You rarely see horned larks perching anywhere but on the ground. To view horned larks, drive back roads and highways and watch for large numbers of the birds flushing up from roadsides at the approach of a vehicle. If you walk up to a group on the ground you may see only a dozen, then flush a hundred, so well are their sandy-colored backs camouflaged against the plain ground.

Agricultural fields provide additional habitat that has allowed this species to expand its range and population in the last hundred years. Widespread in North America, horned larks are the most common song-bird in much of the Great Basin. They are highly gregarious when not nesting, gathering in flocks of hundreds to thousands. In spring, males engage in wild, twisting midair chases; individual birds may rise hundreds of feet into the air, singing a cascade of tinkling notes, then plummet back to earth. Females build nests in simple depressions and raise one or two broods. When disturbed, females fly low and far away from their nests as a distraction.

Living on the ground fully exposed to the elements has its risks. Nests fall prey to weasels, ground squirrels, and snakes, or suffer in bad storms. Adults must also keep an eye out for prairie falcons, their main enemy.

When and Where to See Them: Widespread permanent residents of the Great Basin, especially in areas with sparse vegetation and patches of bare ground. Easily found in winter around agricultural areas but can be observed at any elevation.

Singing male horned larks sometimes sit on elevated perches (top), but they are more often associated with the ground, like this female (bottom).

CLIFF SWALLOW
Petrochelidon pyrrhonota
(Gk *petra*, rock; Gk *chelidon*, swallow. Gk *pyrrhos*,
flame-colored; Gk *notos*, back)

Eye-catchers: The cliff swallow stands out among swallows with its pale, glaring forehead, visible even at a distance. Note the light orangish rump as the bird turns and flies away.

Natural History: With long, pointed wings, swallows are master aerialists. Much of their day is spent in elegant flight, darting and swooping with tiny mouths opened wide to catch an endless supply of small flying insects. Their legs and feet are greatly reduced in size and strength to allow this marvelously developed flying capacity.

Cliff swallows are an abundant and familiar bird. Formerly nesting on remote, rocky cliffs, they have dramatically expanded their range by utilizing human structures. Nowadays it is common to see large colonies of their densely clustered gourd-shaped nests on bridges and buildings. Cliff swallows use these same sites each year and often repair fragile mud nests. Early in the breeding season, the cliff swallow focuses on building a secure nest of mud pellets mixed with saliva.This requires up to 1,200 trips to nearby sources of mud.

Around these communal mud pits, the highly social cliff swallows engage in noisy activity, courting, copulating, and gathering mud all at once. This same frenzied noise continues at the nesting colony, as densely packed neighbors squabble with each other and their mates. They steal fresh mud pellets from neighbors' nests and, later in the season, they sneak into each other's nests to lay eggs. They even carry eggs in their bills from their own nest to drop them quickly into the nests of unsuspecting neighbors. To protect against this theft and parasitism, members of a pair take turns guarding the nest while their mate collects mud and food.

When and Where to See Them: Arrives in late spring in great numbers and quickly begins nesting throughout the Great Basin. Look for nests on cliffs, bridges, and buildings where there is a nearby supply of mud and flying insects. Starts gathering in flocks and heading south in July and August.

A moment's pause at a popular mud hole

A small hole allows entrance into the cliff swallow's mud nest.

ROCK WREN
Salpinctes obsoletus
(Gk *salpinctes,* a trumpeter. L *obsoletus,* indistinct, without clear markings)

Eye-catchers: The rock wren appears dull gray above, with subtle white spots, and is whitish below. It frequently bobs its head and sings in a mixture of buzzes and trills as it explores crevices and creeps, mouselike, across rocky surfaces. The **canyon wren,** a close cousin, also lives in rocky areas but has a pure white throat and cinnamon-colored body.

Natural History: Wherever there are barren rocky outcrops, from sea level to 14,000 feet, you are bound to find *Salpinctes,* the trumpeter, brightening rock arenas and stone ramparts with echoing refrains. Of all the breeding birds in the Great Basin, no other occupies such a broad elevation range. Rock wrens seem oblivious to temperature and climate, so long as they have crevices and holes to poke around in. With great, constant energy, they scramble in and out of narrow cracks where they capture insects and spiders with their long, probing bills. When alarmed, they nervously bob their heads and scold with a buzzy *ti-keer* call. Their repertoire is greatly varied, with over one hundred versions of their song. These songs seem characteristic of desolate, rocky places and evoke strong sentiments in many listeners.

One of the great mysteries of this little-studied bird is its construction of stone paths that lead to its nest. No one has determined why this diminutive bird exerts so much energy laying down hundreds of stones (some so large it is hard to imagine the bird moving them) around its nest site. Sometimes the path is built several feet away from the nest, sometimes other handy materials besides stones may be used, and sometimes the path grows into a wall that makes it difficult for the parents to get in and out of the nest. Watch for these curious paths when you are in rocky areas.

When and Where to See Them: Most abundant and widespread wren in the Great Basin, found around rocky areas. Common from April through September, with a few remaining in protected canyons during winter.

Rock wren

Canyon wren

SAGE THRASHER
Oreoscoptes montanus
(Gk *oros,* a mountain; Gk *scoptes,* a mimic. L *montanus,* mountain)

Eye-catchers: An ashy brown, robin-size bird that sits conspicuously on high perches while singing, the sage thrasher is shy and ground loving otherwise. At close range, a short, straight bill and streaky breast distinguish it from other thrashers and from the similar northern mockingbird; at a distance it appears uniformly pale gray. Its tail is long, with white spots at the corners, and the bird frequently raises and lowers it while perching. The thrasher also holds up its tail for balance when running on the ground. Its flight is strong and direct, at shrub-top level.

Natural History: The sage thrasher's scientific name is misleading, for this is not so much a bird of mountains as one of sagebrush-covered valleys and mesas. There it brightens desert mornings with its loud, cheery, warbling song. The male's bright singing is accompanied by prominent, energetic courtship flights, in which it flies in a deeply undulating, circular route over the sagebrush. Although males sing energetically during courtship early in the season, they fall silent once they begin helping tend eggs in the nest. Good luck if you look for the sage thrasher when it's not singing; they are shy birds that prefer to run on the ground or fly low between dense shrubs.

Sage thrashers capture most of their food—grasshoppers, beetles, and other large insects—on the ground. Sage thrashers are one of the few birds that feed heavily on the destructive Mormon cricket. In late summer, after the young birds have left the large thorny nests, flocks gather to feed openly on fruiting shrubs in preparation for migration.

When and Where to See Them: Found anywhere sagebrush dominates, from valley floors up mountain slopes to an elevation where junipers and mountain mahogany become abundant. One of the first birds of sagebrush habitats to return in spring; common from April to September, with a few stragglers staying through winter.

*The sage thrasher is difficult to see except
when males sing from high perches.*

The sage thrasher has a streaked breast and short bill.

BREWER'S SPARROW
Spizella breweri
(Gk *spiza*, a finch; L *-ella*, little. Named to honor Thomas
Brewer, an avid nineteenth-century birder who was highly
regarded by John James Audubon)

Eye-catchers: This streaked brown and buff bird is best recognized by
its *lack* of eye-catching marks, though careful observers will note its finely
streaked crown and thin, white eye ring. What it misses in color it makes
up for in song, variously described as buzzing, trilling, and canary-like.

Natural History: Perhaps the definitive bird of sagebrush habitats,
the Brewer's sparrow dwells at any elevation where sagebrush grows.
Although abundantly widespread and one of the most persistent singers
of the Great Basin, we know little about the natural history of this bird—
perhaps because it drops to the ground and runs off through dense shrubs
when anyone approaches it. Brewer's sparrows are a challenge to identify,
and beginning birdwatchers should feel amply rewarded when they find
their first one. The best time to observe Brewer's sparrows is in late
summer, when they gather in flocks and engage in flock singing. If you
are near the flock, look for the finely streaked crown and thin, white eye
ring, which are hard to detect from a distance.

Brewer's sparrows are exquisitely adapted for life in the desert, meeting
their water needs with a diet of seeds and insects. They can survive on
this diet without water for up to three weeks, and in times of drought
they reabsorb water that would otherwise be lost in their urine or breath.
When the rains return, Brewer's sparrows bathe frequently, often pausing
to sing at length afterwards.

When and Where to See Them: Widespread in the Great Basin,
nearly always in association with sagebrush, from valley floors to mountain crests. Arrives in early May and begins leaving in August, with some
birds wintering at the southern tip of Nevada.

*The Brewer's sparrow is a plain bird that shows
a finely streaked crown and thin eye ring.*

BLACK-THROATED SPARROW
Amphispiza bilineata

(Gk *amphi*, both sides of; Gk *spiza*, a finch, referring to its close relation to other sparrows. L *bilineata*, two-lined)

> **Eye-catchers:** This warm-brown sparrow blends in against desert shrubs until it turns to display a black bib and face mask highlighted by crisp, white lines on each side. Juvenile birds lack the black bib and do not molt into adult plumage until fall, which is unusually late for a songbird.

Natural History: Most birds living in desert environments must find drinking water to compensate for evaporation and excretion losses. The black-throated sparrow, however, meets its water needs by consuming insects and succulent plant material. This adaptation allows the black-throated sparrow to nest in remote desert regions, where there is little competition with birds that must stay closer to water. Here, on arid, inhospitable rocky slopes with sparse cover, the black-throated sparrow reigns supreme and fills the air with its bright, pleasant, tinkling song. When its young fledge and the summer's intense heat overwhelms the desert, the black-throated sparrow begins visiting watering holes. Like other birds, it avoids extreme temperatures by moving into shade, panting, and holding its wings slightly away from its body.

Black-throated sparrows are fairly easy to find, though their distribution is patchy across the region. In the right habitats they can be abundant and conspicuous, hopping and running on the ground or singing from the tops of scattered shrubs. Even a female, frightened off her well-concealed nest, deliberately makes herself visible as she tries to distract the intruder. Many details of the black-throated sparrow's breeding biology remain unknown, however. During winter, black-throated sparrows gather in mixed sparrow flocks in deserts of the Southwest.

When and Where to See Them: Present in the Great Basin from May to September, with a few birds wintering at the southern end of the region. Breeds on rocky, open slopes around hot valleys and in salt desert scrub among greasewood and shadscale. Numbers may vary from year to year, depending on rainfall and food availability.

Black-throated sparrow

SAGE SPARROW
Amphispiza belli

(Gk *amphi,* on both sides; Gk *spiza,* a finch. Named for John Bell, a naturalist who accompanied Audubon on his journey up the Missouri River)

Eye-catchers: If you catch a glimpse of this secretive bird, notice the contrast of a gray head against a brownish body. Other marks include a white eyebrow, eye ring, and mustache stripe, a black spot on the breast, and a streaky appearance. This bird constantly flicks its long tail.

Natural History: Though common in sagebrush habitats, the sage sparrow is only "watchable" during late spring, when males sing their weak, tinkling *tsit tsit, tsi you, tee a-tee* songs from the tops of shrubs. At other times, sage sparrows hide among dense shrubs, scurrying on the ground like mice. When alarmed they simply run off, only occasionally hopping atop a bush to scope out the threat. Their long tails, which they carry cocked when on the ground, provide balance and maneuverability while they run.

This hidden lifestyle makes it difficult to learn much about sage sparrows. In many areas we probably overlook them, particularly in winter, when males do not sing. It is surprising, however, that sage sparrows ignore large tracts of usable habitat and, where birds do settle, they either bunch their territories up or scatter them widely in seemingly random patterns. We know little about the behavior and responsibilities of males and females around the nest site.

Sage sparrows arrive at their territories in spring already pair-bonded, and quickly set to nesting. Nests are close to or on the ground among shrub cover. Females sit very still on the nest when threatened but at the last minute drop to the ground and scamper off. By June, family groups become common, as parents and young wander and prepare for migration.

Insects figure prominently in their summer diet, but their winter diet consists of seeds, particularly those of annual grasses.

When and Where to See Them: Sagebrush flats and valleys below 7,000 feet. Also found in other shrub and chaparral habitats. Some individuals stay year-round, but many northern populations head for the southern Great Basin, where they are abundant during winter.

A close look at a sage sparrow reveals a gray head against a brown body.

WESTERN MEADOWLARK
Sturnella neglecta
(L *sturnus,* a starling; L *-ella,* little. L *neglecta,* neglected,
so named by Audubon because early ornithologists failed
to separate it from the eastern meadowlark)

Eye-catchers: The western meadowlark is a short-tailed, plump inhabitant of open areas, including grasslands and fields. This bird is well camouflaged from behind but is as brilliant yellow as a ray of sunshine from the front. In flight, the tail appears triangular with prominent white sides.

Natural History: The ability of human language to describe birdsong is stretched thin when it comes to western meadowlarks. Different authors have made various attempts to translate the bubbling, flutelike song that gushes forth from this bird as *Hip! Hip! Hurrah! boys, three cheers!; Oh, yes, I am a pretty-little-bird; I cut'im clean off, I cut'im clean off;* or *U-tah's a pretty place.* Like other grassland birds that lack prominent singing perches, male meadowlarks announce their presence with loud, clear songs. When courting, males jump or fly into the air, or sing from low bushes or fence posts to prominently display their bright yellow undersides. While females have the same plumage as males, they probably identify themselves to males by behavioral differences so as to avoid being mistaken for competing males.

Meadowlarks nest in grasslands and meadows, though they use shrubby areas if there is enough grass in which to conceal their ground nests. Females build grassy domes over their nests, and may approach secretly through dense, grassy tunnels to prevent being observed by predators. While on the eggs, females will sit tight until practically stepped on, to avoid drawing attention to the nest.

The long, stout bill of the meadowlark serves as a digging tool for flipping over dirt clods and probing loose soil for insects and seeds. At times, this bird feasts heavily on the eggs of Mormon crickets.

When and Where to See Them: Common and widespread inhabitant of open areas, grasslands, and fields. Mainly a permanent resident, though numbers decrease in winter. May wander onto high mountain slopes in late summer, but breeds and winters primarily in valleys.

Western meadowlark in full song

Returning to the nest with food

Alpine habitat on Steens Mountain, Oregon

Center left: Rugged high country along east rim of Steens Mountain, Oregon

Center right: Mountain mahoga̶ limber pine–ephedꞁ community in Gosꞁ Mountains, Nevadꞁ

Scattered pines on sagebrush-covered foothills

BIRDS OF MOUNTAINS
AND FOOTHILLS

Slopes climbing above hot desert valleys are home to pinyon pine and juniper woodlands, usually referred to simply as "pinyon-juniper woodlands." This is the definitive forest of the Great Basin. Higher mountain ranges support smaller patches of other conifer species, including ancient bristlecone pines. A few ranges stretch above timberline and support alpine tundra or tundralike conditions.

GOLDEN EAGLE
Aquila chrysaetos
(L *aquila*, eagle. Gk *chrysos*, golden; Gk *aetos*, eagle)

Eye-catchers: With a 7-foot wingspan and a massive body, this dark, soaring bird of deserts and mountains is hard to miss. In good light, adults show a golden hue on the back of the head. Young birds have conspicuous white patches on each wing and at the base of their tails.

Natural History: Long feared and misunderstood, the golden eagle is making a comeback after decades of persecution. The golden eagle voraciously consumes rabbits and ground squirrels, and when rodents are abundant in agricultural areas these eagles become common as well. The nesting cycle of the golden eagle responds strongly to the small mammal population, and many eagles forego nesting when rabbit or ground squirrel populations are low. It takes a lot of food to feed two baby eagles and if the parents cannot provide enough for two mouths, the older and larger eaglet will kill its smaller sibling.

In winters of abundant food, a pair of eagles begins courtship in January or February. Courtship involves circular soaring and roller-coaster flights, diving down and swooping back up. A male will often dive towards his mate, who rolls momentarily upside down in midair as he passes near. Pairs stay together for life and use one huge, bulky nest repeatedly, or alternate among several nests over the years. Nine times out of ten, nests are on remote cliff ledges. Although nests, which weigh as much as a ton, take a tremendous amount of energy to construct, the adults readily abandon the site if disturbed by humans in an early stage of nest building or egg laying.

The golden eagle is a formidable hunter. With 1-inch-long talons and powerful attack dives, it can kill anything from insects to adult deer, either alone or in tandem with its mate. In the Great Basin, its primary food is jackrabbits, but it feeds on carrion whenever possible.

When and Where to See Them: Widespread resident, but most common near mountain ranges. Numbers may increase in winter, as migrants from northern areas join local residents, with movement tied to availability of food supplies.

Adult golden eagles show beautiful golden highlights (captive bird).
Inset: White wing patches are visible on juvenile golden eagles.

CHUKAR
Alectoris chukar

(Gk *alektor,* a cock. Skt *cakora,* a partridge; also *chukar* for its calls)

Eye-catchers: The chukar is plump and vaguely chickenlike, with bright red bill and legs. Its vividly barred sides and black necklace stand out against sandy gray plumage. If suddenly flushed, a covey explodes into the air and heads downhill, alternating short glides with rapid wing beats.

Natural History: This Old World partridge from the eastern Mediterranean region and Middle East was introduced in forty-two states and six Canadian provinces, but only in the arid West of the United States has it persisted. In areas like the Great Basin it finds conditions resembling its ancestral home. The chukar may also feel at home in the region because two vigorous introduced weeds in the Great Basin—cheatgrass and Russian thistle—also harken from the Old World. Hunters pursue huge numbers of this colorful, secretive partridge, making it the chief upland game bird of the Great Basin.

Chukar reveal their presence with trademark *chuk-karr* and *chuk-chuk-chuk-chuk* calls that ring loudly in rocky canyons. A determined search with binoculars may detect a solitary male standing lookout from a large boulder while his covey feeds discreetly below. They are shy and avoid humans in areas where they are hunted.

Coveys of up to forty birds feed on rocky slopes where they can easily spot predators and launch into flight if threatened. They move continually, calling with a resonant chuckling, feeding on seeds, grains, and insects. Surprisingly agile, they run rapidly, and can walk up steep rock faces. At night, a covey roosts among rocks and shrubs, often crouching tail to tail in a watchful circle with all birds facing outward.

During hot, dry weather, this species is limited to areas with daily access to drinking water, and the chukar spends most of its day foraging as it walks to and from a local watering hole. Coveys loiter near water in the late afternoon before heading back to secure hillside roosts.

When and Where to See Them: Common resident about rimrock and arid, shrub-covered slopes at low to mid-elevations. Not found in dense forests. In winter, may travel downslope from areas with heavy snowfall to locate snow-free areas where seeds are easier to find. Wide population fluctuations in response to range conditions.

Vivid side barring and red bill are evident on chukars. —Arnold Small photo

BROAD-TAILED HUMMINGBIRD
Selasphorus platycercus
(Gk *selas*, light; Gk *phoros*, bearing. Gk *platys*, broad;
Gk *kerkos*, tail)

Eye-catchers: The most distinctive feature of this bird is auditory, not visual. Males make a loud, metallic, high-pitched buzzing whistle with their wings as they fly. Females are silent, and look much like many other female hummingbirds except for their conspicuously large tails with rufous patches. Both sexes are metallic green above, but the male has a rose pink throat patch.

Natural History: Though it may not seem so to a casual observer, the mountains of the Great Basin are more closely allied with the Rocky Mountains than with the Sierra Nevada. Plant distributions reflect this and so does the distribution of a few birds, including broad-tailed hummingbirds. This definitive bird of the Rocky Mountains nests throughout the Great Basin, right up to the foot of the Sierra Nevada.

In the high mountains these hummingbirds stay close to streams, arriving in May after the flowers have begun blooming. Males arrive first and defend their territories with great vigor. Any bird, regardless of size, is bombarded when it trespasses onto a male's territory. The combination of furious charges and the ever present whistle of their wings is more than enough. This same energy is directed at nesting females, who find it difficult to feed themselves and sometimes abandon their nestlings rather than starve to death.

A narrowed tip on the outermost feather of each wing generates the male's unique whistling sound. You can hear this sound over the rushing water of nearby mountain streams. When you visit their mountain homes you may find it difficult to locate the producers of these loud, buzzing whistles but, if you do, the reward of seeing a broad-tailed hummingbird makes the search worthwhile.

When and Where to See Them: Found through summer months on many Great Basin mountain ranges, though much less common to the west. Common near streams, but wander onto adjacent dry slopes in places with abundant wildflowers. Generally arrives in late March and stays into September.

Male broad-tailed hummingbird

Female broad-tailed hummingbird

RED-NAPED SAPSUCKER
Sphyrapicus nuchalis
(Gk *sphyra*, a hammer; L *picus*, a woodpecker. NL *nuchalis*, of the neck, referring to the red nape)

Eye-catchers: The small, red patch on the back of the head is diagnostic, though hard to see if the bird is moving about or facing you. Females have a white chin and males have a red one.

Natural History: Throughout summer in the higher mountain ranges, you can find neat rows of horizontal holes drilled by sapsuckers in the bark of aspens, willows, and other trees. Any set of fresh holes, still oozing sap, is a sure sign of sapsucker activity. This sap is a major food source. Unlike other woodpeckers, the tongues of sapsuckers are specially adapted to drinking sap, being soft and fringed with drinking strawlike tubules instead of being hardened and spearlike. Pairs of sapsuckers vigorously defend their "sap wells" against theft by visiting repeatedly to check on each set of holes. Many other birds, particularly warblers and hummingbirds, steal sips of sap whenever possible or eat insects attracted to the sweet sap. Sapsuckers also feed heavily on insects and are adept at catching them in midair.

Sapsuckers prefer forests with a component of aspens for excavating nest cavities. Older aspens with decaying centers under a tough outer layer of bark are excellent cavity trees.

Three species of sapsuckers regularly inhabit the Great Basin, with the red-naped sapsucker being perhaps the most widespread. This species is closely associated with the Rocky Mountains and is therefore more common on the eastern side of the Great Basin. Conversely, the **red-breasted sapsucker,** with an all-red head, is a bird of the Sierra Nevada and the western edge of the Great Basin. The attractive **Williamson's sapsucker,** whose males are predominantly black with a yellow belly, has a poorly known but apparently localized distribution over the entire region.

When and Where to See Them: Breeds in higher mountain ranges, particularly in areas with aspens or riparian habitat. May wander to tree line in late summer, and during migration can be found in low-elevation valleys. During winter, any of the three sapsuckers may remain at low-elevation sites, including individuals from adjacent mountain ranges and ones from northern regions.

Male red-naped sapsuckers are all red on the throat.

Female red-naped sapsuckers have a white chin.

NORTHERN FLICKER
Colaptes auratus

(Gk *kolapto,* to chisel or peck with the bill. L *auratus,* ornamented with gold, referring to the eastern form, which has a yellow wash on its wings)

Eye-catchers: You can recognize this bird in flight, even at a great distance, by its white rump patch and red-hued wings. At rest, the black crescent bib and black-spotted belly are distinctive.

Natural History: Noisy and common, flickers are familiar to many. In spring, their loud courtship calling, vigorous displays, and occasional choice of tin roofs and house siding as drumming sites make them especially easy to locate. Spring courtship includes chases, face-offs, and long series of loud, rolling *wek-wek-wek-wek* calls. Two birds facing each other on a branch tilt their bills up, spread their wings and tail to show off their red-shafted feathers, and bob their heads repeatedly. Often they scuttle across the bark like crabs, vying for position and scrambling from branch to branch.

Once pairs are established, they settle down to reclaim a nesting cavity from the previous year or to excavate a new one. Small owls, kestrels, and other birds that do not construct their own nest holes may take over old flicker cavities. Flickers frequently nest in cottonwoods and willows near streams, or in aspens on mountain slopes, but they use any site where there are trees. The female lays eggs on a bed of fresh wood chips and both sexes incubate, with the male reportedly taking the night shift.

Flickers are unique among North American birds because 45 percent of their diet consists of ants; as many as five thousand may be consumed at a sitting. More than any other woodpecker, they spend much of their time on the ground, using their long bills to stir up ant nests and probe for prey. They also feed on beetles, wasps, grasshoppers, and many wild fruits and berries.

When and Where to See Them: Widespread, from valley floors to timberline. In migration, may be seen crossing sagebrush flats and other unexpected areas. Winter populations vary dramatically, depending on availability of fruits and berries and snow cover on the ground. Northern populations move south in winter, or gather in valleys until April or May when snows melt at higher elevations.

A red cheek patch distinguishes male northern flicker (top) *from female* (bottom).

GRAY FLYCATCHER
Empidonax wrightii

(Gk *empis,* a gnat; Gk *anax,* king; hence, "king of the gnats."
Named for its discoverer, Charles Wright, botanist on the
Pacific Railroad Survey of 1853–56)

Eye-catchers: Recognize this long-tailed, long-billed flycatcher of sagebrush deserts by its pale, almost silvery, gray coloration, by its white belly and two white wing bars, and especially by its habit of persistently twitching, or dropping, its tail downward.

Natural History: Identifying small flycatchers in the genus *Empidonax* (often referred to as "empids") has long been the bane of birdwatchers. Fortunately, the gray flycatcher, the most common and widespread flycatcher in the Great Basin, is relatively easy to identify. As late as the 1920s, however, ornithologists still disagreed on the identifying characteristics of this mystery bird. Prominent ornithologists routinely confused the gray flycatcher with its close cousin, the dusky flycatcher, and they did not discover its breeding grounds in the Great Basin until fifty years after the bird was first collected by Charles Wright.

Flycatchers belong in the catchall category that many people call "little brown birds." Flycatchers differ from vireos, warblers, sparrows, or other small brown birds by their feeding behavior of flying out from exposed perches to catch insects in midair. The gray flycatcher is unusual among flycatchers for its habit of capturing many insects close to the ground or on low plants. It may exhibit this behavior because it lives in areas where much of the vegetation is low and sparse.

Often the gray flycatcher's vigorous song, a bright *chi-bit* followed by a fainter high-pitched *cheep,* is the first thing that draws your attention to this inconspicuous bird as you wander through the sagebrush.

When and Where to See Them: Widespread during migration, but stays primarily in the company of sagebrush when breeding. Prefers open pinyon-juniper woodlands where trees are shrubby, or dry washes where sagebrush can grow nearly as tall as a small tree. Stays longer in the Great Basin than many other small migrants and can be found late April through September.

Gray flycatchers hunt from exposed perches.

PINYON JAY
Gymnorhinus cyanocephalus
(Gk *gymnos,* naked; Gk *rhinos,* a nose. Gk *kyaneos,* dark blue;
Gk *kephale,* a head)

Eye-catchers: The pinyon jay is a bluish bird whose short tail gives
it a stocky appearance. In flight, it looks more like a small crow than
a jay. A long, stout bill, large size, and flocking tendency distinguishes
it from other blue-colored birds.

Natural History: Anyone who spends time in pinyon-juniper woodlands of the Great Basin will soon be familiar with this vocal resident
and its pensive, mewing calls. Highly social birds, pinyon jays commonly
form noisy, chattering groups that work their way through the forest in
search of pinyon pine seeds or insects. When feeding on the ground, a
flock moves in a curious leapfrogging motion like a rolling wave, as birds
at the rear of the flock continuously fly in front of the leading birds.
During these feeding bouts, a few birds stand lookout on high perches
to warn of danger.

In late summer, pinyon jays begin burying tens of thousands of pinyon
pine seeds in preparation for the scarce times of winter. They have a remarkable ability to relocate these caches, but those they miss will sprout
into the next generation of pinyon pines, thus ensuring future food crops.
An absence of feathers around their nostrils helps them avoid getting
dirty as they collect seeds from the pitchy cones, and gives them their
scientific name "naked nose." A bumper crop of seeds directly triggers
breeding behavior in males because it indicates abundant food for next
year's young.

In early spring, members of a flock nest together in loose colonies.
After the eggs hatch, a flock begins "nursery visits," an unusual behavior
where birds check neighbor's nests to examine quality, location, and the
health of the young. We can wonder if these highly intelligent birds learn
from each other's mistakes and triumphs in this way.

When and Where to See Them: Range overlaps year-round with
pinyon pine and juniper trees in most areas. In winters when pinyon
seed crops are poor, large flocks will wander nomadically over vast areas
in search of food.

Pinyon jay

CLARK'S NUTCRACKER
Nucifraga columbiana
(L *nucis*, nut; L *frag*, to break. NL *columbiana*, referring to the Columbia River area where the species was discovered by Lewis and Clark)

> **Eye-catchers:** Half the size of a crow, Clark's nutcracker has a striking black-and-white wing and tail pattern that is most conspicuous when the bird is in flight. The nutcracker has a loud, grating *kraaw* call and a long, stout bill for a bird of its size.

Natural History: Clark's nutcracker and pines are an inseparable pair—where you find one you typically find the other. In the Great Basin, Clark's nutcrackers closely associate with limber, bristlecone, pinyon, and whitebark pines on the high mountain ranges. These pines have large, nutritional seeds on which nutcrackers subsist throughout the year. Nutcrackers depend on pines for food, but pines also depend on nutcrackers to collect and disperse their seeds.

Starting in late summer, as cones mature, nutcrackers collect huge numbers of seeds to bury in shallow caches. Each bird pries apart cones with its long, crowbarlike bill, stuffs a hundred seeds at a time into a pouch under its tongue, and flies off to a sunny, exposed hillside where winter snows will not get too deep. Over several weeks each bird stores up to thirty-five thousand seeds in thousands of small caches. These "pantries" keep the bird alive until the following year's harvest, and it is the many forgotten or unneeded caches that sprout into the next generation of trees.

In late February, with snows still falling and temperatures below freezing, nutcrackers begin building deep, thick-walled nests and laying eggs. Contrary to what you might expect, they select nest sites on cold slopes with the deepest snowpacks. Deep snow signals a site out of the wind, and harsh winter winds would mean death to a bird sitting all day on a nest. Parents feed young birds stored seeds until they can fly, then family groups move to higher elevations for the summer.

When and Where to See Them: Resident bird on mountain ranges throughout the Great Basin, though some winters descending into desert zones if seed crops are poor. Summers spent at high elevations; fall and winter in pinyon pine forests at lower elevations.

*Clark's nutcrackers are a common sight around
mountain campgrounds and picnic areas.*

VIOLET-GREEN SWALLOW
Tachycineta thalassina
(Gk *tachys,* swift; Gk *kineo,* to move. Gk *thalassina,*
sea green color)

Eye-catchers: In good light, the male violet-greeen swallow shows a stunning purple and green sheen with a hint of golden wash. It has a pure white underside, with patches of white extending over the eye, also onto the sides of the rump. Females are duller than males, while juveniles are sooty brown and similar to the juveniles of other swallows.

Natural History: Cleaving the air in skillful flight, swallows are among the most entertaining birds to watch. The violet-green swallow, with its velvety colors and trusting familiarity, is a perennial favorite. People commonly put out nest boxes to attract this species to homes and ranches.

Violet-green swallows are widespread in valleys during spring migration, feeding on insects about water. However, most soon head into the mountains to nest in rock crevices and tree cavities, sites more common at higher elevations. Around cliffs they nest in the company of white-throated swifts and cliff swallows, but when it comes to tree cavities they have to battle a number of competitors for possession of these highly limited sites. Not surprisingly, they seem to prefer nesting on cliffs.

Strong, swift fliers who spend most of the day on the wing, violet-green swallows often nest in remote sites much farther from water than other swallow species. It is no problem for them to travel several miles to find food, and if storms cover the mountains they show up to feed in the valleys. After their young fledge, swallows gather in valleys, feeding around water and lining up on wires by the hundreds. These fall congregations tarry through August into September, then begin their long journey to Mexico and Central America.

When and Where to See Them: Common both as a migrant and a breeding species, with many passing through the Great Basin on their way north and south. Residents nest mainly in the mountains, particularly around rock faces or in tree cavities near clearings and meadows. Migrants return quite early in the spring and many die if cold storms prevent them from finding food in March. Present from late March to September.

Male violet-green swallow

Female violet-green swallow at a nest cavity

MOUNTAIN CHICKADEE
Poecile gambeli

(Gk *poikilos,* many-colored. Named for William Gambel, an ornithologist who collected and wrote about California birds in the 1840s)

Eye-catchers: The mountain chickadee is a small, energetic, gray bird with a black throat and cap. Its key field mark is a white eyebrow, which unfortunately is reduced on some individuals and hard to see.

Natural History: It seems a miracle that small birds can survive frigid winter temperatures, but survive they do. Mountain chickadees winter high in the mountains and can be one of the most numerous birds at such elevations. How does this insect-eating bird secure sufficient amounts of food in such cold weather? Chickadees survive because they have a thick coat of feathers and manage to find a continuous supply of insect eggs and larvae among the needles of conifers. One of their tricks involves peeling down the sides of conifer needles, like peeling a banana, to expose hibernating larvae within each needle. During years of insect outbreaks, chickadees may subsist entirely on this diet. They supplement their diet with conifer seeds.

The gregarious mountain chickadee often forms small flocks, frequently with other species, but as the breeding season approaches pairs split off to establish territories. Breeding occurs at relatively high elevations, mainly from the top edge of pinyon-juniper woodlands up to timberline (roughly 7,000 to 10,000 feet). They seek lush conifer forests and old woodpecker holes for nesting sites, but will nest in other habitats if they find a suitable site. Females sit tight while incubating, perhaps to defend their eggs against chipmunks, and will lunge and hiss vigorously like a snake if directly threatened. The large brood of about seven hungry chicks keeps both parents busy collecting food through the summer. In late summer and fall, the adults remain close to their territories while young birds wander upslope and downslope on their own. Birds that remain at high elevations for winter may be primarily adults who stay near their territory and sleep at night in protective nest holes.

When and Where to See Them: Common year-round residents in high-elevation conifer forests. May also be found in pinyon-juniper woodlands; some in valleys during winter.

Mountain chickadees are distinguished by their white eyebrow (top) and are commonly found in conifers (bottom).

JUNIPER TITMOUSE
Baeolophus griseus
(Gk *baios*, small; Gk *lophos*, crest. NL *griseus*, gray)

> **Eye-catchers:** This bird makes up for its small, plain gray appearance with lively behavior, reflected in its tiny crest: sometimes jaunty and comical, sometimes perky and fierce, sometimes flopped loosely back.

Natural History: Known until recently as the plain titmouse, this bird has undergone a radical identity shift, with newly assigned common and scientific names. Ornithologists now distinguish the Great Basin form from its cousin, the oak titmouse, which lives west of the Sierra Nevada. Researchers based this decision on detailed studies of differences in behavior, voice, and habitat between the two forms. The juniper titmouse resides exclusively in pinyon-juniper woodlands throughout the Great Basin.

Pairs remain together for years on the same territory, which both sexes defend rigorously year-round, even to the extent of chasing away their young as soon as they can fend for themselves. On this territory of 3 to 12 acres, the titmouse pair reigns supreme, and little escapes the birds' vigilance or enduring inquisitiveness. They quickly converge on any activity on their territory, cock their heads from side to side to check out the situation, then, as needed, launch into vociferous complaint or settle back into their routine.

Juniper titmice spend their day hammering open seeds, probing into cracks, prying up flakes of bark, and hopping among branches looking for insects. Their activity is always acrobatic, punctuated with loud, clear *pee-to pee-to pee-to* whistles. They also have a chickadee-like *tsick-a-dee-dee* call in their variable repertoire. In spring, the female selects a natural cavity or old woodpecker hole to line with nesting material. Once on the nest she rarely leaves, and the male brings her a steady supply of food until the eggs hatch.

When and Where to See Them: Lives almost exclusively in pinyon-juniper woodlands, where the evergreen foliage provides year-round cover and food supply. Favors stands with some old trees that have decayed cavities for nesting. Those that show up in other habitats in late fall or winter may be young birds without territories, or ones pushed out by bad weather or a poor food crop.

*The juniper titmouse can raise and lower
its crest, depending on its activities.*

MOUNTAIN BLUEBIRD
Sialia currucoides
(Gk *sialis*, a kind of bird. Sp *curruca*, the linnet; Gk *oides*, like, resembling)

Eye-catchers: The male is a gorgeous, sky blue bird, while the female is brownish gray with blue tints. Both sexes lack the red breast of the **western bluebird,** a less common species in the Great Basin.

Natural History: This bird is the state bird for both Nevada and Idaho, an apt symbol for a land of vast, wide-open spaces. True to their name, mountain bluebirds reside in mountains, though they descend into valleys during winter. At all elevations they favor open country for feeding, with a preference for meadows, rock fields, and burned areas. Because perches can be rare or absent in open habitats, these birds have evolved long wings that enable them to hover. From midair, or sometimes from perches, they swoop down onto the ground to catch insects.

Migrating mountain bluebirds return by mid-February, making them one of the earliest arrivals. They push northward and into the mountains as soon as snows start to clear, but a late winter can cause them to bunch up on lower slopes, waiting to nest. They build nests in abandoned wood-pecker holes or natural cavities adjacent to open areas at mid- to high elevations. Many mountain bluebirds nest in aspen forests because aspens are usually riddled with holes and are next to mountain meadows.

Some people report hearing mountain bluebirds sing a soft, robinlike song that begins in full darkness and continues till sunrise, but these birds are mainly silent and many expert birdwatchers have never heard this song. More often heard are thin *few* calls.

By late summer, family groups and small flocks head downslope and southward. Those that stay through winter switch to a diet of fruits and berries, including those of junipers and Russian olives, when insects are no longer available.

When and Where to See Them: While nesting, found on mountains from 7,000 to 12,000 feet in a variety of open habitats. Most head south by autumn, but some stay behind in valleys through winter, their number depending on food supplies.

Male mountain bluebird shows a little white around its lower belly.

Female mountain bluebird nesting in an aspen

Juvenile mountain bluebirds are speckled underneath.

This male western bluebird shows off its red breast.

TOWNSEND'S SOLITAIRE
Myadestes townsendi
(Gk *myia,* a fly; Gk *edestes,* anteater. Named for John K.
Townsend, who first collected this bird near the Columbia River)

Eye-catchers: Townsend's solitaire is a long, slender, brownish gray bird with an alert, upright posture and a clearly visible eye ring. In flight, it shows white outer tail feathers and a buffy patch on the wing.

Natural History: For decades after its discovery by John Townsend, the famous naturalist, the Townsend's solitaire remained a mystery. Years passed before ornithologists found another specimen, and there was an ongoing debate about how to classify the species. One of its old names, Townsend's flycatching thrush, captures this indecision. Eventually taxonomists assigned it to the solitaires, a group of Mexican birds, but many details about its breeding biology remain unknown.

The Townsend's solitaire has an unusual schedule, for it is one of the only birds that sings in and defends a winter territory. After breeding in high mountain forests all summer, Townsend's solitaires move to valleys and foothill slopes in September. Each bird's goal is to find a dependable patch of berries that will last the winter. Some years Townsend's solitaires must range widely in search of juniper berries, their favored food in the Great Basin. Once the birds locate patches, they vigorously sing and squabble until they have established a network of winter territories. The clear, sweet, warbling song of the Townsend's solitaire seems an expression of wild, open spaces. You may also hear another call, a creaky whistle resembling the call of a pygmy owl.

Come spring, solitaires return to the high country, where they nest on or near the ground and switch from a diet of berries to one of insects. Their nests often resemble a tuft of windblown material caught in a crevice. A hanging apron of loose fibers constructed below the nest adds to the haphazard appearance, which may help disguise the nest from predators.

When and Where to See Them: Rare to abundant at lowland sites from September to May, almost certain to be found wherever there are junipers with large berry crops. Inhabits open forests of mountains through summer.

The white eye ring is perhaps the Townsend's solitaire's most conspicuous mark, but also note the small, buff patch on wing (below).

AMERICAN ROBIN
Turdus migratorius
(L *turdus*, a thrush. L *migro*, to wander, giving LL *migrator,* wanderer)

Eye-catchers: Males are red breasted with brownish backs and dark hoods; females and young birds are similar though duller in color. Very young birds are spotted underneath.

Natural History: American robins are a familiar sight in the Great Basin and throughout North America. Prior to agricultural development in the Great Basin, these birds spent their summers in moist areas on mountain ranges. They have adapted well to modern changes and are now common in summer on lawns, in gardens, and in fields. Although common, their fiercely combative nature keeps them widely dispersed during the nesting season.

Robins can be far more obvious in winter, when flocks of hundreds or thousands wander together in search of food. Depending on the year's wild berry and fruit crops, robin populations range from extremely abundant to virtually absent. In the Great Basin, robins feed heavily on juniper berries through the winter. On hillsides with a good crop of juniper berries, the air rings with the calls and scolds of feeding robins. These flocks roost together at night, returning daily to a good food site until they have picked it clean, then leaving to search for another food crop.

With the first signs of spring, males return to the areas of their previous years' territories and sing their loud, cheery songs. Females soon follow and build deep, mud-lined nests. Robins typically raise two broods, with the male tending the first batch of youngsters while the female incubates the second set of eggs. During these summer months, their primary habitat requirement is soft, rich soil where they can find a wealth of worms and insects on which to feed. They also require mud for building nests. By late autumn, their diet switches to berries and fruits, and they utilize a broad variety of habitats.

When and Where to See Them: Common and widespread. Found in moist areas in summer, nomadic during the winter.

Male American robin

Female American robin

Robins build tidy, mud-lined nests.

YELLOW-RUMPED WARBLER
Dendroica coronata
(Gk *dendron*, tree; Gk *oikeo*, to dwell or inhabit.
L *coronatus*, crowned)

Eye-catchers: During all seasons, the *chip* call note and flashing yellow rump are diagnostic. Breeding males are vividly patterned, although females and winter birds are dingy gray and streaked. Always look for the yellow rump to identify this bird. There are two different forms: the "myrtle warbler" has a white throat, and the "Audubon's warbler" has a yellow throat.

Natural History: During the cold, gray days of fall, long after most songbirds have headed south, the yellow-rumped warbler continues to flit among bare branches in search of food. This hardy warbler lingers late in the year and arrives early in the spring, with a few remaining through winter. This is remarkable because warblers typically feed on insects, which are difficult to find in the colder months. Yellow-rumped warblers solve this problem by foraging for berries, seeds, and even tree sap from sapsucker holes. In particular, they have evolved the ability to produce enzymes that digest wax, allowing them to consume waxy berries.

After spending the winter in small, loose groups of gray, dingy birds, male yellow-rumps blossom into full color in March. Birds partway through this molting process look rather comical, as if they were formed of a patchwork of fabric scraps, but a male in final breeding plumage is quite beautiful. After molting, males move upslope to their breeding grounds in aspen stands and coniferous forests, and begin singing slow, warbling songs that accelerate at the end. When courting, males fluff out their feathers to highlight their yellow patches as they follow females. Nests of yellow-rumped warblers are unique in frequently having a row of feathers woven into the rim, so that they lean inward and partly hide the eggs. Females forage lower than males, remaining close to the nest while males feed and stand watch from high perches.

When and Where to See Them: Moves up onto mountain slopes in March and April as soon as weather allows. Breeds in mountain forests and roams widely in late summer and fall until cold weather drives it back downslope. Can be scarce to fairly common through winter at lower elevations, though most head south to milder climates.

Even in dull, winter plumage, the yellow rump is diagnostic.

The breeding male yellow-rumped warbler is vividly colored.

BLACK-THROATED GRAY WARBLER
Dendroica nigrescens
(Gk *dendron,* a tree; Gk *oikeo,* to dwell, inhabit. L *nigrescens,* becoming black)

Eye-catchers: The black-throated gray warbler shows more extensive black markings than the similar mountain chickadee (page 132), and has streaky underparts and two white wing bars. At close range, you can see a tiny yellow spot in front of the eye. Males have a richer black color and larger black throat patch than females.

Natural History: This western warbler is one of the most common birds in pinyon-juniper woodlands, but we know surprisingly little about its diet, breeding biology, and nesting behavior. Though sometimes shy and retiring, black-throated gray warblers feed deliberately and persistently about needle clusters at the ends of branches. During this methodical foraging, they lean over and peer under leaves, or stretch up to gain different viewpoints. Only occasionally do they hover and flycatch in the manner of other warblers.

Among Great Basin warblers, black-throated gray warblers live in some of the warmest, driest habitats—pinyon-juniper woodlands on mountain and foothill slopes. Their buzzy *weezy weezy weezy weezy-weet* song is a characteristic sound of these woodlands. Despite omnipresent vocalizations, we rarely find their cupped nests. Females often build their nests far out on a horizontal branch, but do an excellent job of hiding its location as they come and go.

Black-throated gray warblers commonly accompany small mixed flocks of feeding birds moving through the woodlands. Common associates include common bushtits, mountain chickadees, and other warblers.

When and Where to See Them: Distribution limited to pinyon-juniper woodlands and stands of mountain mahogany on lower mountain slopes, with a preference for warm sunny locales. Found from early May into September.

A black throat patch distinguishes the male black-throated gray warbler (top) from the female (bottom).

WILSON'S WARBLER
Wilsonia pusilla

(Named in tribute to Alexander Wilson, the "father of American ornithology." L *pusillus,* very small)

Eye-catchers: This pretty little yellow warbler with a black cap has eyes that appear large, giving the bird a gentle expression.

Natural History: Although primarily a bird of Canada's forests, the Wilson's warbler finds suitable breeding habitat at high elevations in the Great Basin. In addition, tremendous numbers migrate across the region, making it one of the most common and visible songbirds in May and August. At all times these warblers brighten brushy thickets with their color and activity, appearing and disappearing as they flit about within the dark inner recesses. They prefer thickets and rarely stray to high or exposed perches. Even singing males remain within the confines of dense vegetation, making it hard to locate the owner of the loud, staccato series of *chips* that serves as a song.

Wilson's warblers find their optimal nesting sites near streams, lakes, and wet meadows, building the nests on or near the ground. Young birds are dull-colored but molt into an adultlike plumage by the time they leave the nest. Many aspects of this bird's life in the Great Basin remain unstudied.

Wilsonia warblers belong to a group of flycatching warblers that have broader, flatter bills than other warblers and that show rictal bristles (see western kingbird on page 88). These features help them catch insects, especially those in flight. Unlike other flycatching birds, however, Wilson's warblers rarely dart out into the open air to chase insects. Instead, they snatch most of their prey from leaves within the interior of tangled thickets.

When and Where to See Them: Widespread, common, and found almost anywhere during migration. Breeding birds restricted to moist, brushy thickets in high valleys and in mountains.

The male Wilson's warbler (top) has a more extensive black cap than the female (bottom).

WESTERN TANAGER
Piranga ludoviciana

(*Piranga,* a native name for a South American bird.
NL *ludoviciana,* of Louisiana. First collected by Lewis and Clark
in Idaho, at that time part of the Louisiana Purchase)

Eye-catchers: This is perhaps the Great Basin's most vividly colored bird, with males arrayed in fluorescent reds and yellows. Females, juveniles, and nonbreeding males lack the intense reddish orange color, but all show two pale yellow wing bars. A thick, chunky bill helps distinguish females from superficially similar female Bullock's orioles (page 64).

Natural History: The Great Basin's human population is certainly blessed to have this tropical bird visit the area, even for only a short breeding season. The long journey from Central America gives the tanager little time in its summer home, with some beginning the return trip even as the last stragglers start settling in.

During spring migration, large numbers congregate in many habitats, adding color to the landscape. All too soon, however, they head up into high mountain forests for their final stop. Here, they occupy open, coniferous forests and nest high in tall trees. Males sing throughout the breeding season in a song much like the American robin, but hoarser and more somber; both sexes utter a *pit-ic* call.

Slow, deliberate behavior characterizes western tanagers. While foraging, they scan the foliage and air unhurriedly, sometimes sitting motionless for long periods, tilting their heads from side to side. They prefer to feed among large branches open to the air so they can flash out easily, if necessary, to catch flying insects. At the same time, dense foliage seems important to these birds for hiding places, perhaps because their gaudy plumage makes them a ready target for *Accipiter* hawks.

Insects, especially wasps and ants, figure prominently in tanagers' diets during the breeding season, but as summer wanes tanagers consume larger amounts of ripening wild fruits.

When and Where to See Them: Breeds in coniferous forests at high elevations on most Great Basin mountain ranges, sometimes in aspen groves and stands of trees mixed with mountain mahogany. May wander upslope after breeding, and shows up almost anywhere during migration. Arrives in May and leaves by the end of September.

*Male
western
tanager*

*Female
western
tanager
drinking*

*Male
western
tanager
bathing*

GREEN-TAILED TOWHEE
Pipilo chlorurus
(L *pipo*, to chirp or peep. Gk *chloros*, green; Gk *oura*, tail)

Eye-catchers: This bird is normally secretive but striking when observed in good light. A reddish crown, crisp white throat patch, and distinct cheek stripe contrast sharply against the gray body. Its wings and tail are greenish with yellow highlights, its tail is long and rounded at the tip, and it has stout, strong legs.

Natural History: If you sit quietly near brushy thickets on mountain slopes, you will soon hear this ubiquitous, though secretive, bird of the Great Basin. In spring its bright songs are among the most characteristic sounds of the mountains, starting with clear whistles, ending with a buzzy trill, and frequently incorporating elements of neighboring birdsongs.

If you sit long enough you will be rewarded by the sight of this beautiful bird perched high on a shrub or tree, scouting out the terrain and singing. They are even more conspicuous when scuffling in the shade of shrubs, kicking aside leaf litter in search of insects and seeds. Avoiding predators is one of the reasons they keep to dense vegetation. Green-tailed towhees prefer low, spreading shrubs that cover open ground, where they run about like chipmunks with their tails carried over their backs. This behavior, called the "rodent run," helps them avoid human observers and, one assumes, predators as well.

Many aspects of this species' life history remain unknown. Females build well-concealed nests on or near the ground, and they quickly run off if disturbed, making it even more difficult to locate their nests. When distressed, towhees will utter catlike meows of complaint or remain silent. This species' short wings keep them from making long flights, so their northward migration in spring consists of a series of short journeys over a period of several months.

When and Where to See Them: Found in brushy, mountain habitats composed of mixed shrubs and widely scattered trees. In late summer, may wander upslope prior to migration. Arrives toward the end of April, remaining into September.

*It takes a good look to appreciate all
the green-tailed towhee's field marks.*

LAZULI BUNTING
Passerina amoena
(L *passer,* sparrow; L *-ina,* like. L *amoenus,* lovely)

Eye-catchers: The male is a brilliant, blue jewel of a bird with white wing bars and an orange band across his breast. The female has subtle coloration and is difficult to identify when by herself. Look for a bluish body tinge and orangish chest on a warm brown bird.

Natural History: The lazuli bunting is a stellar example of the avian scheme whereby males are loud and conspicuous and females are camouflaged and secretive. The male's loud, clear warbling song leads your eye to the songster perched on high branches, where his blue feathers stand out in the desert landscape like a fluorescent beacon. The female stays hidden in the dense vegetation where she is seldom seen as she feeds and nests.

Lazuli buntings favor streamside thickets of willows, wild rose, and other shrubs in mountain valleys at mid-elevations across the Great Basin. The development of irrigation channels has allowed this species to expand its range into formerly arid regions, including lowland valleys. Like other finches with thick, seed-eating bills, lazuli buntings feed on seeds and grains, especially those of grasses. They often feed by flying out to grass seed heads that they then carry, still attached to flexible stalks, to the ground or to a close perch where they can pry out individual seeds. They supplement this diet with large-bodied insects such as grasshoppers.

In order to raise two broods by summer's end, a pair cooperates in caring for the young. The female cares for the first brood until the young leave the nest, then the male takes over while the female builds a new nest and lays another clutch of eggs.

When and Where to See Them: Male arrives first, in early to mid-May, to begin setting up territories. Found in a variety of habitats and elevations but always near water; prefers sites with dense shrubs in a patchy mosaic with open grassy areas. Following breeding, frequently wanders in groups to high elevations before leaving the region during September.

Female lazuli bunting (top) shows hints of the male's (bottom) vibrant blue and orange coloration.

SUGGESTED READING

The Birder's Handbook: A Field Guide to the Natural History of North American Birds. Paul R. Ehrlich, et al., editors. New York: Simon and Schuster. 1988.

Birds of the Great Basin: A Natural History. Fred A. Ryser, Jr. Reno: University of Nevada Press. 1985.

Birds of Malheur National Wildlife Refuge, Oregon. Carroll D. Littlefield. Corvallis: Oregon State University Press. 1990.

The Birds of Nevada. J. R. Alcorn. Fallon, Nevada: Fairview West Publishing. 1988.

A Field Guide to Western Birds. 3rd Edition. Roger Tory Peterson. Boston: Houghton Mifflin Company. 1990.

National Geographic Society Field Guide to the Birds of North America. 3rd Edition. Shirley L. Scott, editor. Washington, D.C.: National Geographic Society. 1999.

The Sagebrush Ocean: A Natural History of the Great Basin. Stephen Trimble. Reno: University of Nevada Press. 1989.

Southern Nevada Birds: A Seeker's Guide. Carolyn Kitchel Titus. Las Vegas: Red Rock Audubon Society. 1991.

Stokes Field Guide to Birds: Western Region. Donald and Lillian Stokes. Boston: Little, Brown and Company. 1996.

Utah Birds. William H. Behle and Michael L. Perry. Salt Lake City: Utah Museum of Natural History. 1975.

GREAT BASIN
BIRDING HOT SPOTS

Bear River Migratory Bird Refuge. Located on the northeast shore of the Great Salt Lake. The refuge is one of the major migratory stops on the Pacific Flyway, with great numbers of waterfowl and shorebirds. Adjacent upland habitats attract desert, foothill, and mountain birds.

Goshute Mountains. Located on the eastern border of Nevada just south of Wendover. The best site in the western United States for migrating fall raptors. Over a thousand raptors a day can be seen in mid-September from an observation post run by Hawkwatch International of Salt Lake City.

Great Basin National Park. This remote, little-visited national park is located on the eastern border of Nevada. Provides easy access to high-elevation forests, alpine tundra, and a diversity of mountain species, including the scarce three-toed woodpecker.

Lahontan Valley Wetlands. Located one hour east of Reno, Nevada. Scarcely visited region with two areas—Stillwater National Wildlife Refuge and Carson Lake—offering Nevada's premier birding opportunities. Hundreds of thousands of waterfowl and shorebirds visit during migration. Summer birds include thousands of pelicans and ibis. Nevada's largest concentration of bald eagles gathers here in winter.

Malheur National Wildlife Refuge. Located in the southeast corner of Oregon and established by Theodore Roosevelt in 1908. One of the most important stopping points on the Pacific Flyway, with immense numbers of waterfowl in early spring. Malheur is a famous site for rare migrants and has a rich diversity of birds throughout the year.

Mono Lake. Located in California on the east slope of the Sierra Nevada. In late summer and early fall, Mono Lake hosts over one million eared grebes and tens of thousands of phalaropes. The majority of California's California gulls nest at Mono Lake.

Pahranagat National Wildlife Refuge. Located north of Las Vegas in southern Nevada. Good site for raptors in winter. Lakes and marshes attract waterfowl and shorebirds.

Ruby Lake National Wildlife Refuge. Located in eastern Nevada, southeast of Elko. Freshwater marshes and open waters attract large numbers of waterbirds, including white-faced ibis, trumpeter swans, redheads, canvasbacks, and black terns.

INDEX

—Barbara Hall photo

ABOUT THE AUTHOR

David Lukas, a native of Oregon, began memorizing field guides by their pictures before he was old enough to read, and he has been an avid birdwatcher for more than twenty years. An English graduate from Reed College in Portland, Oregon, he has published his writing in *Wild Bird, Birding,* and *Orion* magazines. From his home in the foothills of the Sierra Nevada, Lukas regularly journeys into the Great Basin, where he leads birdwatching and natural history tours for such groups as the Audubon Society, The Nature Conservancy, and Elderhostel.

We encourage you to patronize your local bookstores. Most stores will order any title that they do not stock. You may also order directly from Mountain Press by mail, using the order form provided below, or by calling our toll-free number and using your Visa or MasterCard. We will gladly send you a complete catalog upon request.

Some other titles of interest:

____An Introduction to Northern California Birds		$14.00
____An Introduction to Southern California Birds		$14.00
____Birds of the Central Rockies		$14.00
____Birds of the Pacific Northwest Mountains		$14.00
____Desert Wildflowers of North America		$24.00
____Geology Underfoot in Death Valley and Owens Valley		$16.00
____Geology Underfoot in Southern California		$14.00
____OWLS Whoo are they?		$12.00
____Roadside Geology of Northern California		$15.00
____Roadside History of California	paper $18.00 / cloth	$30.00
____Roadside Plants of Southern California		$15.00
____Sagebrush Country *A Wildflower Sanctuary*		$14.00
____Sierra Nevada Wildflowers		$16.00
____Watchable Birds of California		$18.00
____Watchable Birds of the Great Basin		$16.00
____Watchable Birds of the Rocky Mountains		$14.00
____Watchable Birds of the Southwest		$14.00

Please include $3.00 per order to cover shipping and handling.

Send the books marked above. I enclose $_____

Name_____

Address_____

City/State/Zip_____

☐ Payment enclosed (check or money order in U.S. funds)

Bill my: ☐ VISA ☐ MasterCard Expiration Date:_____

Card No._____

Signature _____

MOUNTAIN PRESS PUBLISHING COMPANY
P. O. Box 2399 • Missoula, MT 59806
Order Toll Free 1-800-234-5308 • Have your Visa or MasterCard ready.
e-mail: mtnpress@montana.com • website: www.mtnpress.com